Preston L(

Beginner
ENGLISH

2nd Edition

For Persian Speakers

Preston Lee Books

No unauthorized photocopying

All rights reserved. No part of this publication may be reproduced, stored in a retrieval system, or transmitted, in any form or by any means, without the prior permission in writing of Preston Lee Books.

This book is sold subject to the condition that it shall not, by the way of trade or otherwise, be lent, resold, hired out, or otherwise circulated without the publisher's prior consent in any form of binding or cover than that in which it is published and without a similar condition including this condition being imposed on the subsequent purchaser.

Copyright © 2023 Matthew Preston, Kevin Lee
All rights reserved.
ISBN: 9798854651998

These 44 lessons have been taken from

Preston Lee's Beginner English 100 Lessons

CONTENTS

Lesson 1: My family خانواده ی من — Page 8
Lesson 2: My pencil case جامدادی من — Page 12
Lesson 3: In the classroom در کلاس — Page 16
Lesson 4: The weather آب و هوا — Page 20

Test 1 Lesson 1 - 4 — Page 24

Lesson 5: Places مکان ها — Page 26
Lesson 6: Sports ورزش ها — Page 30
Lesson 7: At the zoo در باغ وحش — Page 34
Lesson 8: Colors رنگ ها — Page 38

Test 2 Lesson 5 - 8 — Page 42

Lesson 9: Activities فعالیت ها — Page 44
Lesson 10: Food & Drinks غذا و نوشیدنی — Page 48
Lesson 11: At the fruit market در بازار میوه — Page 52
Lesson 12: Shapes شکل ها — Page 56

Test 3 Lesson 9 - 12 — Page 60

Lesson 13: At the supermarket در سوپرمارکت   Page 62
Lesson 14: At the ice cream shop در فروشگاه بستنی   Page 66
Lesson 15: In the refrigerator در یخچال   Page 70
Lesson 16: Jobs شغل ها   Page 74

| Test 4 | Lesson 13 - 16 | Page 78 |

Lesson 17: Names نام ها   Page 80
Lesson 18: More places مکانهای بیشتر   Page 84
Lesson 19: Meats گوشت   Page 88
Lesson 20: Vegetables سبزیجات   Page 92

| Test 5 | Lesson 17 - 20 | Page 96 |

Lesson 21: At school در مدرسه   Page 98
Lesson 22: School subjects موضوعات مدرسه   Page 102
Lesson 23: Chores کارها   Page 106
Lesson 24: At the toy store در فروشگاه اسباب بازی   Page 110

| Test 6 | Lesson 21 - 24 | Page 114 |

Lesson 25: In the kitchen در آشپزخانه   Page 116
Lesson 26: In the toolbox در جعبه ابزار   Page 120
Lesson 27: Transportation حمل و نقل   Page 124
Lesson 28: Clothes لباس ها   Page 128

| Test 7 | Lesson 25 - 28 | Page 132 |

Lesson 29: More clothes لباس های بیشتر		Page 134
Lesson 30: In the living room در اتاق نشیمن		Page 138
Lesson 31: In the bathroom در حمام		Page 142
Lesson 32: In the bedroom در اتاق خواب		Page 146

Test 8	Lesson 29 - 32	Page 150

Lesson 33: Around the house در اطراف خانه		Page 152
Lesson 34: Hobbies سرگرمی		Page 156
Lesson 35: Countries کشورها		Page 160
Lesson 36: Landscapes مناظر طبیعی		Page 164

Test 9	Lesson 33 - 36	Page 168

Lesson 37: Everyday life زندگی روزمره		Page 170
Lesson 38: Languages زبان ها		Page 174
Lesson 39: Pets حیوانات خانگی		Page 178
Lesson 40: Fast food فست فود		Page 182

Test 10	Lesson 37 - 40	Page 186

Lesson 41: At the cinema در سینما		Page 188
Lesson 42: Music موسیقی		Page 192
Lesson 43: Feelings احساسات		Page 196
Lesson 44: The calendar تقویم		Page 200

Test 11	Lesson 41 - 44	Page 204

Answers	Test 1 - 11	Page 206

Lesson 1: My family

خانواده ی من

Who is she?
She is my baby sister.

| Section A | Words |

1. mother
مادر
2. grandmother
مادر بزرگ
3. sister
خواهر
4. baby sister
خواهر کوچولو
5. aunt
عمه-خاله

6. father
پدر
7. grandfather
بابا بزرگ
8. brother
برادر
9. baby brother
برادر کوچولو
10. uncle
دایی- عمو

| Section B | Make a sentence |

Who is <u>she</u>?

She is my <u>mother</u>.

She isn't my <u>aunt</u>.

Who is <u>he</u>?

He is my <u>father</u>.

He isn't my <u>uncle</u>.

Note: isn't = is not

Section C — Make a question

Is <u>she</u> your <u>mother</u>?

Yes, she is. / No, she isn't.

Is <u>he</u> your <u>father</u>?

Yes, he is. / No, he isn't.

Alternative: **Yes, he is my <u>father</u>.**

Section D — Learn a verb

see – seeing – saw – seen دیدن

He **sees** my father on Fridays.

I will be **seeing** him this afternoon.

My brother **saw** you yesterday.

I haven't **seen** that movie yet.

Section E — Learn an idiom

Like one of the family

Meaning: To be like a person in one's family.

"Our dog is treated *like one of the family*."

| Section F | Write |

Trace and write the words

1. _____ is _____?

She is my _____. She _____ my grandmother.

2. Who _____ he?

He is _____ father. _____ isn't _____ brother.

3. Who _____ _____?

She _____ my grandmother.

4. Who _____ _____?

He _____ _____ grandfather.

5. Is she _____ sister?

Yes, _____ is.

6. Is _____ your brother?

No, he _____.

7. Is _____ _____ mother?

Yes, _____ _____.

8. Is _____ _____ father?

_____, _____ _____.

Section G   Let's have fun

My family!

Find the words!

```
c j o b j t d c z b g g r o v k
o i j m w d o g f a j r k s s q
q d e g q l z t c b z a q c u o
u w n r c e o z s y i n t t t v
n f f a t h e r o b a d y s y r
c d l n b h j m u r x f d v t q
l z a d m g g y e o x a c m n v
e h p m o t h e r t z t j y t f
f u e o v q q f d h e h b x s n
n z v t u x l w j e z e k o u v
t a a h s i s t e r o r y a l r
t o u e y v s h b r o t h e r j
j n n r u d o s x j v t y k y o
j b t y t d b a b y s i s t e r
```

~~mother~~	brother
father	baby sister
grandmother	baby brother
grandfather	aunt
sister	uncle

Lesson 2: My pencil case

جامدادی من

What is this?
It is an eraser.

Section A — Words

1. a pencil
مداد
2. an eraser
پاک کن
3. glue
چسب
4. a pencil sharpener
مداد تراش
5. whiteout
لاک غلط‌گیری
6. a pen
خودکار
7. a ruler
خط کش
8. tape
نوارچسب
9. a marker
ماژیک
10. a crayon
مداد شمعی

Section B — Make a sentence

What is this?

It is <u>a pencil</u>.

It isn't <u>a marker</u>.

What are these?

They are <u>pen</u>s.

They aren't <u>crayons</u>.

Note: aren't = are not

Section C — Make a question

Is this <u>an eraser</u>?

Yes, it is. / No, it isn't.

Are these <u>ruler</u>s?

Yes, they are. / No, they aren't.

Alternative: **Yes, they are rulers.**

Section D — Learn a verb

buy – buying – bought – bought خریدن

I will **buy** some pencils for you.

My sister was **buying** a new ruler.

My father **bought** an eraser.

My mother hasn't **bought** some glue yet.

Section E — Learn an idiom

Cross your fingers

Meaning: To wish for luck.

"*Cross your fingers* and hope this marker has ink."

| Section F | Write |

Trace and write the words

1. What _____ this?

It is _____ pencil. _____ isn't _____ marker.

2. What _____ these?

They are _____. They _____ pencil _____.

3. What _____ _____?

It _____ whiteout. It isn't an _____

4. What _____ _____?

They _____ markers. _____ aren't _____.

5. Is _____ _____ eraser?

Yes, _____ is.

6. Is _____ a _____ sharpener?

No, _____ _____.

7. Is _____ a crayon?

No, _____ isn't.

8. _____ _____ rulers?

Yes, _____ _____.

Section G | Let's have fun

My pencil case!

Unscramble the words!

1. encpil — pencil
2. enp
3. relru
4. eugl
5. reshrapne cpneli
6. arerse
7. emrakr
8. hwteituo
9. yocarn
10. ptae

Lesson 3: In the classroom

در کلاس

What are these?
These are old books.

Section A — Words

1. chair
   صندلی
2. blackboard
   تخته سیاه
3. poster
   پوستر
4. globe
   کُره جهان
5. clock
   ساعت
6. desk
   میز مطالعه
7. whiteboard
   تخته سفید
8. bookshelf
   قفسه کتاب
9. computer
   کامپیوتر
10. book
    کتاب

Section B — Make a sentence

What is this?

This is a <u>big</u> <u>chair</u>.

This isn't a <u>small</u> chair.

What are these?

These are <u>small</u> <u>desk</u>s.

These aren't <u>big</u> desks.

Learn: big, small, new, old

Section C — Make a question

Is the <u>blackboard</u> <u>big</u>?
Yes, it is. / No, it is <u>small</u>.

Are the <u>desks</u> <u>new</u>?
Yes, they are. / No, they are <u>old</u>.

Alternative: **Yes, the desks are new.**

Section D — Learn a verb

look – looking – looked – looked نگاه کردن

Please **look** at the blackboard.

They are **looking** at the whiteboard.

My father **looked** at your bicycle yesterday.

We have already **looked** at many houses.

Section E — Learn an idiom

Class clown

Meaning: A student who often makes everyone laugh in the classroom.

"Peter is the *class clown*. Even the teacher laughs sometimes."

| Section F | Write |

Trace and write the words

1. What is _____?

This is _____ big _____. This _____ a small chair.

2. What _____ these?

_____ are small _____. These aren't _____ desks.

3. What _____ _____?

This is a _____ globe. _____ isn't an old _____.

4. What _____ _____?

These _____ old books. _____ aren't _____ books.

5. Is _____ blackboard _____?

_____, it _____.

6. Are _____ desks _____?

No, they _____ old.

7. Is the _____ small?

No, _____ is _____.

8. Are the _____ _____?

Yes, _____ _____.

Section G | Let's have fun

In the classroom!

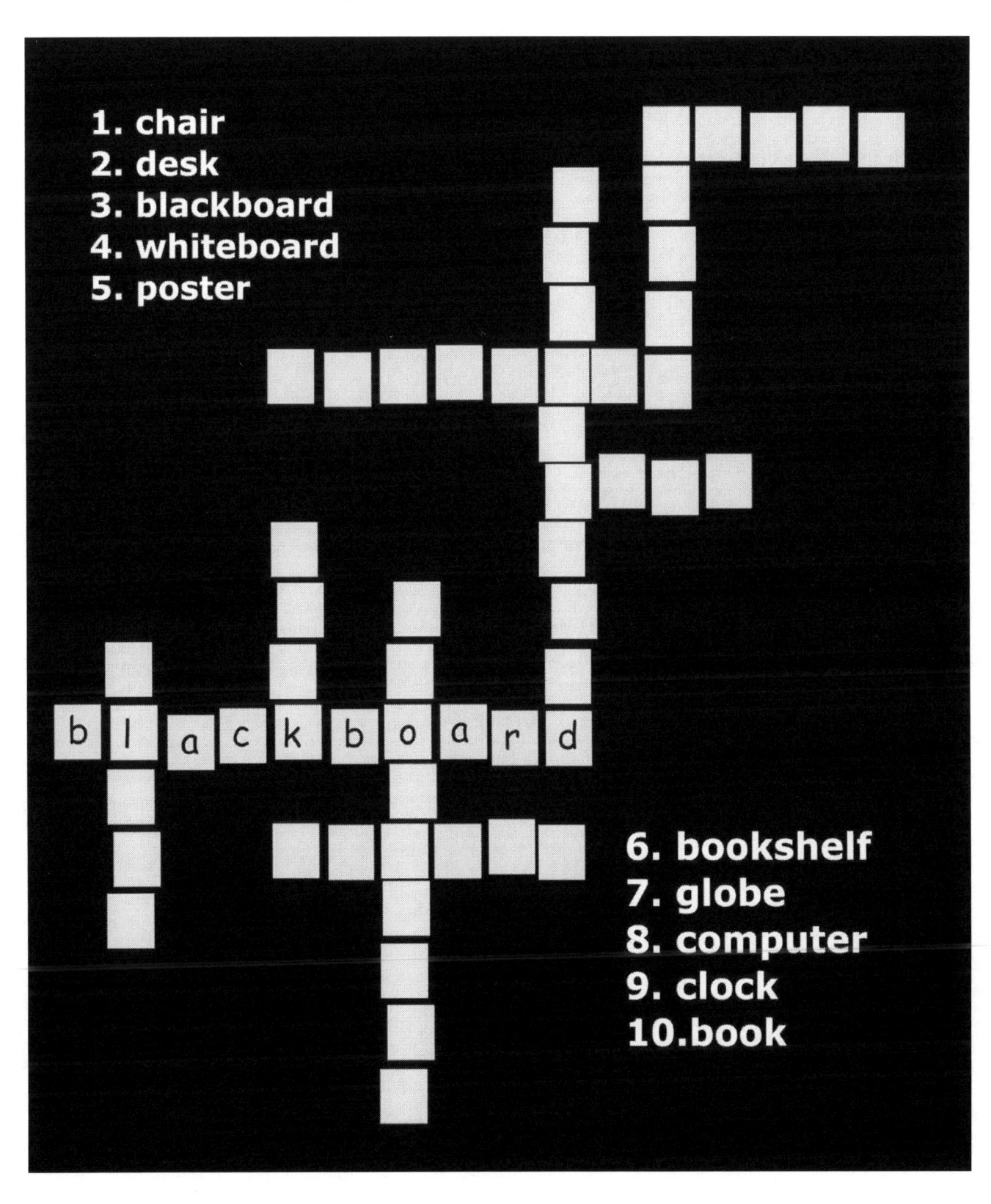

1. chair
2. desk
3. blackboard
4. whiteboard
5. poster

b l a c k b o a r d

6. bookshelf
7. globe
8. computer
9. clock
10. book

Lesson 4: The weather

آب و هوا

How is the weather on Friday?
It is sunny.

| Section A | Words |

1. **snowy**
برفی
2. **sunny**
آفتابی
3. **rainy**
بارانی
4. **windy**
بادی
5. **cloudy**
ابری

6. **hot**
داغ
7. **cold**
سرد
8. **warm**
گرم
9. **cool**
سرد
10. **freezing**
انجماد

| Section B | Make a sentence |

How is the weather on <u>Monday</u>?

It is <u>snowy</u>.

It is not <u>hot</u>.

Alternative: **The weather is snowy.**

Learn: Sunday, Monday, Tuesday, Wednesday, Thursday, Friday, Saturday

| Section C | Make a question |

Is the weather <u>cold</u> on <u>Wednesday</u>?

Yes, it is. / No, it isn't. It is <u>hot</u>.

Is the weather <u>sunny</u> on <u>Sunday</u>?

Yes, it is. / No, it isn't. It is <u>rainy</u>.

Alternative: **Yes, the weather is sunny on Sunday.**

| Section D | Learn a verb |

feel – feeling – felt – felt احساس کردن

My sister always **feels** tired after school.

I'm not **feeling** well.

I **felt** something on the back of my neck.

I haven't **felt** this happy for a long time!

| Section E | Learn an idiom |

It's raining cats and dogs

Meaning: It's raining heavily.

"You can't play outside right now. *It's raining cats and dogs.*"

| Section F | Write |

Trace and write the words

1. How _____ the _____ on Monday?

It is _____. It is _____ windy.

2. _____ is the weather _____ Thursday?

_____ is cloudy. It _____ not _____.

3. How is the _____ _____ Friday?

It is _____.

4. How is _____ _____ _____ Tuesday?

It _____ cold. It is _____ _____.

5. Is the _____ hot?

Yes, it _____.

6. Is _____ _____ windy on Wednesday?

No, it _____. It is _____.

7. Is the _____ _____ on Saturday?

Yes, _____ _____.

8. Is _____ weather _____ _____ Friday?

No, it _____. It is _____.

Section G   Let's have fun

The weather!

snowy   sunny   rainy   windy   cloudy

hot   cold   warm   cool   freezing

Write the words

Sunday	Monday	Tuesday	Wednesday	Thursday	Friday	Saturday
Ra_n_	W_n_y	Cl_u_y	S_n_y	C_ _d	H_ _	W_r_

Circle the correct answer

1. Is the weather cold on Thursday?

   Yes, it is.   No, it's not. It's hot.

2. Is the weather windy on Monday?

   Yes, it is.   No, it's not. It's hot.

3. Is the weather rainy on Wednesday?

   Yes, it is.   No, it's not. It's sunny.

4. Is the weather cold on Friday?

   Yes, it is.   No, it's not. It's hot.

Test 1   Lesson 1 - 4

Write the answer next to the letter "A"

A: ___ **1.** Who ___ she? She is ___ mother.

a. is, my   b. are, her   c. am, his   d. is, me

A: ___ **2.** ___ he your father? Yes, ___ is.

a. Is, she   b. Are, he   c. Is, he   d. Are, she

A: ___ **3.** We ___ a movie now.

a. are seeing   b. seen   c. is seeing   d. saw

A: ___ **4.** "The housekeeper is one ___ the family."

a. off   b. is   c. from   d. of

A: ___ **5.** What are ___? ___ are markers.

a. this, They   b. these, It   c. it, They   d. these, They

A: ___ **6.** Are ___ rulers? No, ___ aren't.

a. it, these   b. them, it   c. these, they   d. this, it

A: ___ **7.** I ___ a pencil yesterday.

a. buy   b. buying   c. bought   d. buys

A: ___ **8.** Tom: "I hope I pass my test." Mary: "___ your fingers."

a. Hold   b. Cross   c. Pull   d. Look at

A: ___ **9.** What ___ these? These are ___ posters.

a. are, those   b. is, small   c. is, old   d. are, big

A: ___ **10.** Is the ___ small? No, it is ___.

a. it, old   b. globe, big   c. chair, desk   d. this, new

A: ___ **11.** He is ___ at the whiteboard.

a. looks   b. looking   c. looked   d. look

A: ___ **12.** "Johnny is the class ___. He's so funny."

a. clown   b. clowned   c. clowning   d. clowns

A: ___ **13.** How is the ___ on Tuesday? It is ___. It is not hot.

a. weather, cold   b. rainy, sunny   c. cool, old   d. hot, rain

A: ___ **14.** Is the weather ___ on Friday? Yes, ___ is.

a. cold, it   b. cold, snowy   c. hot, sunny   d. it, cold

A: ___ **15.** She ___ feel cold.

a. very   b. isn't   c. doesn't   d. do

A: ___ **16.** "Look at the heavy rain. It's raining ___ and ___."

a. lots, water   b. dogs, cats   c. cat, dog   d. cats, dogs

Answers on page 206

Lesson 5: Places

مکان ها

Where is he going?
He is going to the gym.

Section A — Words

1. park
   پارک
2. beach
   ساحل دریا
3. night market
   بازار شب
4. store
   فروشگاه
5. supermarket
   سوپر مارکت
6. restaurant
   رستوران
7. swimming pool
   استخر
8. department store
   فروشگاه بزرگ
9. cinema
   سینما
10. gym
    سالن ورزش

Section B — Make a sentence

Where is <u>she</u> going?

She is going to the <u>park</u>.

She isn't going to the <u>store</u>.

Where is <u>he</u> going?

He is going to the <u>beach</u>.

He isn't going to the <u>cinema</u>.

Section C — Make a question

Is <u>he</u> going to the <u>store</u>?

Yes, he is. / No, he isn't.

Is <u>she</u> going to the <u>supermarket</u>?

Yes, she is. / No, she isn't.

Alternative: **Yes, she is going there.**

Section D — Learn a verb

walk – walking – walked – walked راه رفتن

I **walk** at the park on Sundays.

She will be **walking** to the store tomorrow morning.

My grandmother **walked** to the supermarket last week.

I've never **walked** to the night market before.

Section E — Learn an idiom

Have a change of heart

Meaning: To change your mind about something.

"I've *had a change of heart* about this place. Let's go to another restaurant."

Section F   Write

Trace and fill in the words

1. Where _____ _____ going?

She is _____ to _____ park.

2. Where _____ he _____?

He _____ going to _____ restaurant.

3. Where is _____ _____?

She _____ going _____ the _____.

4. Where _____ he _____?

_____ is _____ to the _____ pool.

5. _____ he _____ to the _____ store?

Yes, _____ _____.

6. Is _____ going _____ the _____ market?

_____, she _____.

7. _____ he _____ to _____ restaurant?

Yes, _____ is.

8. Is she _____ _____ the _____?

No, _____ _____.

Section G | Let's have fun

Places!

1. Where is he going? — Department store

He is going to the department store.

2. Where is she going? — Gym

_____

3. Where is he going? — Restaurant

_____

4. Where is she going? — Supermarket

_____

5. Where is he going? — Cinema

_____

Lesson 6: Sports

ورزش ها

> What are you playing?
> I am playing golf.

Section A — Words

1. basketball
   بسکتبال
2. soccer
   فوتبال
3. badminton
   بدمینتون
4. golf
   گلف
5. hockey
   هاکی
6. cricket
   کریکت
7. tennis
   تنیس
8. baseball
   بیسبال
9. volleyball
   والیبال
10. football
    فوتبال (فوتبال آمریکایی)

Section B — Make a sentence

What are <u>you</u> playing?

I am playing <u>basketball</u>.

I'm not playing <u>football</u>.

What are <u>they</u> playing?

They are playing <u>soccer</u>.

They aren't playing <u>volleyball</u>.

Note: I'm = I am

Section C | Make a question

Are <u>you</u> playing <u>basketball</u>?
Yes, I am. / No, I'm not.

Are <u>they</u> playing <u>soccer</u>?
Yes, they are. / No, they aren't.

Alternative: **Yes, they are going to play soccer.**

Section D | Learn a verb

play – playing – played – played بازی کردن

I **play** basketball at the park on the weekends.

She will be **playing** tennis in the school competition.

My brother and I **played** badminton last night.

My grandfather has **played** golf for a long time.

Section E | Learn an idiom

A good sport

Meaning: Someone who can accept losing or be made fun of.

"We made fun of Johnny, but he was *a good sport* and laughed with us."

Section F — Write

Trace and fill in the words

1. What _____ you playing?

   _____ am _____ basketball.

2. _____ is _____ playing?

   She _____ playing _____.

3. What _____ they _____?

   _____ are playing _____.

4. What _____ they _____?

   They _____ playing _____.

5. _____ you _____ volleyball?

   Yes, _____ am.

6. _____ she _____ football?

   No, _____ isn't.

7. _____ they playing _____?

   Yes, _____ are.

8. _____ you playing _____?

   No, _____ _____.

Section G Let's have fun

Sports!

Connect the sentences

What are you playing? • ————————— • We are playing soccer.

What are they playing? • ————————— • I am playing tennis.

What are you playing? • • He is playing basketball.

What is he playing? • • They are playing baseball.

Are you playing golf? • • No, she isn't.

Is she playing hockey? • • Yes, they are.

Is he playing football? • • Yes, I am.

Are they playing volleyball? • • No, he isn't.

Lesson 7: At the zoo

در باغ وحش

How many lions are there?
There are two lions.

Section A — Words

1. monkey
میمون
2. lion
شیر
3. tiger
ببر
4. rhino
کرگدن
5. bear
خرس
6. penguin
پنگوئن
7. giraffe
زرافه
8. elephant
فیل
9. kangaroo
کانگورو
10. crocodile
تمساح

Section B — Make a sentence

How many <u>monkey</u>s are there?

There is one monkey.

There are <u>three</u> monkeys.

There aren't any monkeys.

Learn: one, two, three, four, five, six, seven, eight, nine, ten

Note: there's = there is

Section C — Make a question

Is there one <u>rhino</u>?

Yes, there is. / No, there isn't.

Are there <u>five</u> <u>bears</u>?

Yes, there are. / No, there aren't.

Alternative: **Yes, there are five bears.**

Section D — Learn a verb

like – liking – liked – liked دوست داشتن

I **like** the kangaroo.

The penguins are **liking** the new fish.

We **liked** the lions best at the zoo yesterday.

The bear hasn't **liked** any of the food we prepared.

Section E — Learn an idiom

Let the cat out of the bag

Meaning: To let someone know a secret.

"He let the cat out of the bag about the surprise party."

| Section F | Write |

Trace and fill in the words

1. How _____ monkeys _____ there?

There _____ one _____.

2. How _____ penguins _____ there?

There _____ _____ penguins.

3. How many _____ are there?

There _____ any _____.

4. How many _____ are _____?

There _____ six _____.

5. Is _____ one rhino?

Yes, _____ _____.

6. Are _____ four _____?

_____, there _____.

7. Is _____ one _____?

Yes, there _____.

8. _____ there four _____?

No, _____ _____.

| Section G | Let's have fun |

At the zoo!

Read and write

ANIMAL	AMOUNT
Monkey	6
Giraffe	
Lion	
Tiger	
Penguin	
Elephant	
Bear	
Kangaroo	
Crocodile	

1. How many monkeys are there?
   There are six monkeys.

2. How many giraffes are there?
   There are four giraffes.

3. How many lions are there?
   There is one lion.

4. How many penguins are there?
   There are seven penguins.

5. How many elephants are there?
   There are two elephants.

6. How many bears are there?
   There is one bear.

7. How many kangaroos are there?
   There are three kangaroos.

8. How many crocodiles are there?
   There is one crocodile.

Lesson 8: Colors

رنگ ها

Section A — Words

1. red
سرخ
2. blue
آبی
3. orange
نارنجی
4. pink
صورتی
5. black
سیاه

6. yellow
رنگ زرد
7. green
سبز
8. purple
بنفش
9. brown
قهوه ای
10. white
سفید

Section B — Make a sentence

What color is this?

It is <u>red</u>.

It isn't <u>purple</u>.

What is your favorite color?

My favorite color is <u>yellow</u>.

My favorite color isn't <u>green</u>.

Note: it's = it is

Section C — Make a question

Is this <u>pencil</u> <u>purple</u>?
Yes, it is. / No, it's <u>blue</u>.

Is your favorite color <u>green</u>?
Yes, it is. / No, it isn't.

Alternative: **Yes, this crayon is purple.**

Section D — Learn a verb

draw – drawing – drew – drawn رسم کردن, نقاشی کشیدن

My uncle can **draw** a green crocodile.

She is **drawing** a black bear.

The teacher **drew** a pink elephant on the blackboard.

I had first **drawn** a brown monkey, but didn't like it.

Section E — Learn an idiom

Feeling blue

Meaning: Feeling unhappy.

"He's *feeling blue* today because he lost the game."

| Section F | Write |

Trace and fill in the words

1. What color is _____?

It _____ green.

2. What _____ your _____ color?

My favorite _____ is _____.

3. What color is _____?

It is _____.

4. _____ is your favorite _____?

My _____ color is _____.

5. Is _____ pencil _____?

Yes, _____ _____.

6. Is _____ favorite _____ pink?

No, it _____.

7. _____ this eraser _____?

No, it's _____.

8. Is _____ favorite color _____?

_____, it _____.

40

Section G Let's have fun

Colors!

1. What color is this? _____. It is yellow.

2. What is your favorite color? _____. My favorite color is green.

3. Is this an orange pencil? _____. Yes, it is.

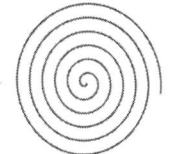

4. Is your favorite color blue? _____. No, it isn't.

| Test 2 | Lesson 5 - 8 |

Write the answer next to the letter "A"

A: ___ **1.** Where ___ she going? She is ___ to the beach.

a. does, going   b. is, going   c. are, go   d. is, go

A: ___ **2.** Is ___ going to the store? Yes, she ___.

a. we, can   b. her, is   c. she, is   d. he, is

A: ___ **3.** Yesterday, they ___ to the cinema.

a. are walk   b. walk   c. walked   d. walking

A: ___ **4.** "I changed my mind about going. I had a change of ___."

a. eyes   b. think   c. clothes   d. heart

A: ___ **5.** What are ___ playing? We ___ playing tennis.

a. you, are   b. we, is   c. they, can   d. she, are

A: ___ **6.** ___ you playing soccer? No, ___ not.

a. Is, she's   b. Are, I'm   c. Can, can   d. Are, he's

A: ___ **7.** They want to ___ baseball.

a. played   b. playing   c. plays   d. play

A: ___ **8.** "We laughed at John, but he was a ___ sport."

a. well   b. good   c. easy   d. difficult

A: ___ **9.** How many ___ are there? There ___ two tigers.

a. tiger, are   b. number, is   c. tiger, is   d. tigers, are

A: ___ **10.** Is ___ one kangaroo? No, there ___.

a. there, isn't   b. number, isn't   c. this, is   d. this, aren't

A: ___ **11.** He ___ the penguins.

a. like   b. liking   c. likes   d. was like

A: ___ **12.** "He told everyone my secret and let the cat ___ the bag."

a. out from   b. into   c. out of   d. out

A: ___ **13.** What is your ___ color? My favorite color ___ purple.

a. best, is   b. best, are   c. favorite, are   d. favorite, is

A: ___ **14.** Is this desk ___? Yes, ___ is.

a. red, they   b. color, pink   c. green, it   d. yellow, he

A: ___ **15.** She can ___ a yellow lion.

a. drawing   b. draw   c. draws   d. drew

A: ___ **16.** "I'm pretty unhappy today. I'm feeling ___."

a. red   b. green   c. color   d. blue

Answers on page 206

Lesson 9: Activities

فعالیت ها

What do you like to do?
I like to read books.

Section A — Words

1. **play piano**
   پیانو زدن
2. **read books**
   خواندن کتاب ها
3. **play video games**
   بازی کردن با بازی های ویدئویی
4. **surf the internet**
   گشت و گذار در اینترنت
5. **take photos**
   عکس گرفتن
6. **watch TV**
   تماشای تلویزیون
7. **sing songs**
   آواز خواندن
8. **study English**
   مطالعه انگلیسی
9. **play cards**
   پاسور
10. **go shopping**
    خرید رفتن

Section B — Make a sentence

What do you like to do?

I like to <u>play piano</u>.

I don't like to <u>read books</u>.

What don't you like to do?

I don't like to <u>sing songs</u>.

I like to <u>watch TV</u>.

Note: don't = do not

Section C — Make a question

Do you like to <u>play video games</u>?
Yes, I do. / No, I don't.

Don't you like to <u>read books</u>?
Yes, I do. / No, I don't.

Alternative: **Yes, I like to read books.**

Section D — Learn a verb

read – reading – read – read خواندن

I can **read** English books.

My sister was **reading** the newspaper this morning.

I **read** a really interesting article last week.

My brother hasn't **read** this book yet.

Section E — Learn an idiom

Shop around

Meaning: To shop at different stores to find the best price.

"You should *shop around* before you buy this piano."

| Section F | Write |

Trace and fill in the words

1. What _____ you like _____ do?

   I _____ to _____ books.

2. What _____ you _____ to do?

   _____ don't like to _____ cards.

3. _____ do you _____ to do?

   I like to _____ _____.

4. What don't _____ like to _____?

   I _____ like to _____ _____.

5. Do _____ like to _____ photos?

   No, I _____.

6. Don't you _____ to go _____?

   Yes, _____ _____.

7. Do _____ like to _____ _____?

   Yes, I _____.

8. Don't you _____ to _____ _____?

   _____, I _____.

Section G | Let's have fun

Activities!

Unscramble the sentences!

> like to / video games / I / play

1. _____.

> I / like to / read books / don't

2. _____.

> I / study English / like / to

3. _____.

> don't / go shopping / I / like to

4. _____.

> like / take / I / photos / to

5. _____.

> the / don't / I / to / like / internet / surf

6. _____.

Lesson 10: Food & Drinks

غذا و نوشیدنی

> How much tea is there?
> There is a lot of tea.

Section A — Words

1. cake
كيك
2. cheese
پنير
3. milk
شير
4. tea
چاى
5. soda
سودا
6. pizza
پيتزا
7. water
آب
8. juice
آب ميوه
9. coffee
قهوه
10. pie
پاى

Section B — Make a sentence

How much <u>cake</u> is there?

There is <u>a little</u> cake.

There isn't any cake left.

How much <u>pizza</u> is there?

There is <u>a lot of</u> pizza.

There isn't any pizza left.

Learn: a little, a lot of

Section C — Make a question

Is there a lot of <u>juice</u>?

Yes, there is. / No, there isn't.

Is there a little <u>water</u>?

Yes, there is. / No, there isn't.

Alternative: **Yes, there is a little left.**

Section D — Learn a verb

want – wanting – wanted – wanted خواستن

I **want** a lot of tea.

Wanting to improve your English takes practice.

They **wanted** a cheese cake, but the shop didn't have one.

My father has **wanted** to eat pizza all week.

Section E — Learn an idiom

Put food on the table

Meaning: To make money for the household expenses.

"I need this job to *put food on the table*."

| Section F | Write |

Trace and fill in the words

1. _____ much juice is _____?

    There is a _____ _____.

2. How _____ coffee _____ there?

    There _____ a lot of _____.

3. How much _____ is _____?

    There is a _____ _____.

4. _____ much _____ is there?

    There isn't _____ milk _____.

5. Is there _____ lot _____ cheese?

    Yes, _____ is.

6. Is _____ a little tea?

    No, there _____.

7. Is there a _____ of _____?

    _____, there _____.

8. Is _____ a little _____?

    No, _____ _____.

| Section G | Let's have fun |

Food + Drinks!

Circle the odd word

1. cake   pizza   cheese   (soda)   pie
2. soda   tea   cake   juice   milk
3. pizza   coffee   cheese   pie   cake
4. pie   soda   water   tea   coffee
5. cheese   cake   tea   pie   pizza
6. pizza   milk   coffee   juice   water
7. cake   juice   cheese   pie   pizza
8. water   soda   milk   juice   cheese

Write the word

1.
2.
3.
4.
5.
6.
7.
8.

Lesson 11: At the fruit market

در بازار میوه

> What do you want?
> I want an apple.

Section A | Words

1. **orange**
   پرتغال
2. **pear**
   گلابی
3. **watermelon**
   هندوانه
4. **strawberry**
   توت فرنگی
5. **cherry**
   گیلاس
6. **lemon**
   لیمو
7. **banana**
   موز
8. **grape**
   انگور
9. **pineapple**
   آناناس
10. **apple**
    سیب

Section B | Make a sentence

What do you want?

I want an <u>orange</u>.

I don't want a <u>banana</u>.

What don't you want?

I don't want a <u>lemon</u>.

I want an <u>apple</u>.

Note: Say *an* for all nouns that begin with a, e, i, o, u.

Section C — Make a question

Is there one <u>pear</u>?

Yes, there is. / No, there isn't.

Are there <u>five</u> <u>grape</u>s?

Yes, there are. / No, there aren't.

Alternative: **Yes, there are five grapes.**

Section D — Learn a verb

need – needing – needed – needed نیاز داشتن

I **need** two watermelons for the picnic.

People **needing** vitamin C should eat more oranges.

Yesterday, I **needed** to buy some apples.

I haven't **needed** to use the heater this year.

Section E — Learn an idiom

A bad apple

Meaning: The one bad person in a good group.

"He is *a bad apple* on this basketball team."

Section F — Write

Trace and fill in the words

1. What _____ you want?

I _____ an apple. I _____ want a pear.

2. What don't you _____?

I don't _____ a cherry. I want an _____.

3. What _____ you want?

I want a _____. I don't _____ _____ lemon.

4. What _____ you _____?

I don't _____ a _____. I want _____ orange.

5. Is _____ one _____?

Yes, there _____.

6. Are _____ seven _____?

_____, there aren't.

7. Is _____ one _____?

No, _____ isn't.

8. Are _____ three _____?

Yes, _____ _____.

Section G Let's have fun

At the fruit market!

| orange | lemon | pear | strawberry | banana |
| watermelon | grape | pineapple | cherry | apple |

1. __orange__
- lemon
- pear
- strawberry
- pineapple
- watermelon
- apple
- cherry
- banana
- grape

2. _____
- apple
- orange
- strawberry
- banana
- pear
- lemon
- grape
- pineapple
- cherry

3. _____
- strawberry
- apple
- orange
- watermelon
- pineapple
- pear
- cherry
- banana
- grape

4. _____
- lemon
- pear
- strawberry
- orange
- watermelon
- apple
- cherry
- banana
- pineapple

5. _____
- lemon
- grape
- strawberry
- pineapple
- watermelon
- apple
- cherry
- orange
- banana

6. _____
- pear
- orange
- watermelon
- banana
- strawberry
- apple
- cherry
- lemon
- grape

7. _____
- grape
- pear
- orange
- pineapple
- watermelon
- apple
- banana
- cherry
- lemon

8. _____
- lemon
- pear
- strawberry
- cherry
- watermelon
- banana
- orange
- pineapple
- grape

Lesson 12: Shapes

شکل ها

> What color is this circle?
> This is a green circle.

Section A — Words

1. **square**
   مربع
2. **circle**
   دایره
3. **star**
   ستاره
4. **heart**
   قلب
5. **octagon**
   هشت ضلعی
6. **triangle**
   مثلث
7. **rectangle**
   مستطیل
8. **oval**
   بیضی
9. **diamond**
   الماس
10. **pentagon**
    پنج ضلعی

Section B — Make a sentence

What color is this <u>square</u>?

This is a <u>red</u> square.

This isn't a <u>purple</u> square.

What color is that <u>triangle</u>?

That is a <u>blue</u> triangle.

That isn't a <u>green</u> triangle.

| Section C | Make a question |

Is this <u>circle</u> <u>green</u>?

Yes, it is. / No, it isn't. It's <u>blue</u>.

Is that <u>rectangle</u> <u>orange</u>?

Yes, it is. / No, it isn't. It's <u>purple</u>.

Alternative: **Yes, that is an orange rectangle.**

| Section D | Learn a verb |

find – finding – found – found پیدا کردن

I can't **find** my keys.

The teacher is **finding** many mistakes in my homework.

I **found** my grandfather's watch.

He still hasn't **found** his workbook.

| Section E | Learn an idiom |

Be out of shape

Meaning: To be unfit or overweight.

"He can't climb this mountain. He *is* really *out of shape*!"

Section F — Write

Trace and fill in the words

1. What _____ is this rectangle?

   This is a _____ rectangle. This isn't a green _____.

2. _____ color _____ that oval?

   _____ is a green _____. That _____ a blue oval.

3. What _____ is _____ diamond?

   This is a _____ diamond. _____ isn't a red _____.

4. _____ color _____ that _____?

   _____ _____ a _____ heart.

5. _____ this _____ purple?

   Yes, _____ is.

6. _____ that octagon _____?

   No, _____ _____. It's pink.

7. Is this _____ _____?

   Yes, _____ _____.

8. _____ that _____ red?

   No, _____ _____. It's _____.

| Section G | Let's have fun |

Shapes!

1. What color is this rectangle?

   This is a blue rectangle.   .

2. What color is this star?

   _____.

3. What color is this circle?

   _____.

4. What color is this oval?

   _____.

5. What color is this diamond?

   _____.

6. What color is this square?

   _____.

7. What color is this pentagon?

   _____.

8. What color is this triangle?

   _____.

Test 3   Lesson 9 - 12

Write the answer next to the letter "A"

A: ___ **1.** What ___ you like to do? I like to ___ piano.

a. does, do   b. is, play   c. are, go   d. do, play

A: ___ **2.** Don't ___ like to play cards? Yes, I ___.

a. we, can   b. you, do   c. he, am   d. you, can

A: ___ **3.** He ___ comic books.

a. read   b. reading   c. see   d. reads

A: ___ **4.** "I think I can find a cheaper price. I'm going to ___ around."

a. buy   b. play   c. shop   d. cost

A: ___ **5.** How ___ pizza is there? There is ___ pizza.

a. many, big   b. much, a lot of   c. small, many   d. much, all

A: ___ **6.** Is ___ a lot of coffee? No, ___ isn't.

a. there, there   b. this, lot   c. them, she   d. it, he

A: ___ **7.** My grandmother ___ a lot of soda.

a. want   b. wanting   c. wants   d. doesn't

A: ___ **8.** "I need that job to put ___ on the table."

a. food   b. money   c. meat   d. milk

A: ___ 9. What ___ you want? I don't ___ a banana.

a. do, try   b. can't, want   c. can, have   d. don't, want

A: ___ 10. ___ there seven cherries? No, there ___.

a. Is, isn't   b. Our, aren't   c. Are, aren't   d. Have, hasn't

A: ___ 11. We ___ eight pineapples.

a. needing   b. needs   c. need   d. is need

A: ___ 12. "He's not a nice guy. He's really a bad ___."

a. tomato   b. orange   c. lemon   d. apple

A: ___ 13. What color is ___ oval? That ___ a purple oval.

a. that, is   b. this, are   c. an, can   d. purple, has

A: ___ 14. Is this ___ blue? Yes, it ___.

a. circle, can   b. heart, does   c. square, is   d. star, blue

A: ___ 15. I can't ___ an orange octagon.

a. finding   b. found   c. find   d. be found

A: ___ 16. "He really needs to get healthy. He's really ___ shape."

a. into   b. taking   c. losing   d. out of

Answers on page 206

Lesson 13: At the supermarket

در سوپرمارکت

What do you want to buy?
I want to buy some bread.

Section A — Words

1. **milk**
   شیر
2. **juice**
   آب میوه
3. **meat**
   گوشت
4. **drinks**
   نوشیدنی ها
5. **vegetables**
   سبزیجات
6. **ice cream**
   بستنی
7. **fruit**
   میوه
8. **bread**
   نان
9. **fish**
   ماهی
10. **pizza**
    پیتزا

Section B — Make a sentence

What do you want to buy?

I want to buy some <u>milk</u>.

I don't want to buy any <u>bread</u>.

What don't you want to buy?

I don't want to buy any <u>ice cream</u>.

I want to buy some <u>fruit</u>.

Learn: some, any

Section C — Make a question

Do you want to buy some <u>juice</u>?
Yes, I do. / No, I don't.

Do you want to buy some <u>fruit</u>?
Yes, I do. / No, I don't.

Alternative: **Yes, I want to buy some fruit.**

Section D — Learn a verb

get – getting – got – gotten گرفتن

I **get** my bread at the supermarket.

He is **getting** some bananas from the fruit market.

Last night, she **got** a pizza for dinner.

We haven't **gotten** any vegetables yet.

Section E — Learn an idiom

A rip off

Meaning: Something is too expensive.

"The supermarket around the corner is *a rip off*."

Section F | Write

Trace and fill in the words

1. What do you _____ to buy?

I want _____ buy _____ fruit.

2. What _____ you want _____ buy?

I don't _____ to buy _____ bread.

3. What _____ you want to _____?

I want to _____ some _____.

4. What _____ you _____ to buy?

I don't want to _____ any _____.

5. Do you want to buy some fish?

Yes, I _____.

6. Do _____ want to _____ some milk?

No, _____ don't.

7. Do you _____ to buy _____ _____?

Yes, I _____.

8. Do you want to _____ some _____?

No, I _____.

64

Section G Let's have fun

At the supermarket!

Read the conversation

Max: What do you want to buy?

Julie: I want to buy some milk.

Max: What don't you want to buy?

Julie: I don't want to buy any meat.

Max: What do you want to buy?

Julie: I want to buy some fruit.

Max: What do you want to buy?

Julie: I want to buy some bread.

Max: What don't you want to buy?

Julie: I don't want to buy any fish.

Max: What do you want to buy?

Julie: I want to buy some vegetables.

Circle the things Julie wants

meat   milk   fruit   fish   vegetables

ice cream   bread   pizza   drinks   juice

Write the things she wants in the shopping cart

1. _____
2. _____
3. _____
4. _____

Lesson 14: At the ice cream shop

در فروشگاه بستنی

Which flavor do you like?
I like mint flavor.

Section A — Words

1. **chocolate**
   شکلات
2. **strawberry**
   توت فرنگی
3. **mint**
   نعنا
4. **raspberry**
   تمشک
5. **cherry**
   گیلاس
6. **vanilla**
   وانیل
7. **coffee**
   قهوه
8. **almond**
   بادام
9. **caramel**
   کارامل
10. **coconut**
    نارگیل

Section B — Make a sentence

Which flavor do you like?

I like <u>chocolate</u> flavor.

I don't like <u>almond</u> flavor.

Which flavor does he like?

He likes <u>vanilla</u> flavor.

He doesn't like <u>raspberry</u> flavor.

Note: doesn't = does not

Section C — Make a question

Do you like <u>strawberry</u> ice cream?

Yes, I do. / No, I don't.

Does she like <u>mint</u> ice cream?

Yes, she does. / No, she doesn't.

Alternative: **Yes, she likes mint ice cream.**

Section D — Learn a verb

have/has – having – had – had داشتن

She **has** coffee ice cream in her refrigerator.

I am **having** mint ice cream instead.

My sister **had** almond ice cream last time.

My father hasn't **had** caramel ice cream yet.

Section E — Learn an idiom

Flavor of the month

Meaning: Something is suddenly popular for a short time.

"This song is just the *flavor of the month*."

Section F — Write

Trace and fill in the words

1. Which _____ do _____ like?

   I like _____ flavor.

2. _____ flavor _____ he like?

   He _____ chocolate _____.

3. Which _____ do you _____?

   I like _____ _____.

4. Which _____ does she _____?

   She _____ _____ _____.

5. Do you _____ vanilla ice _____?

   No, I _____.

6. _____ she like coffee _____ cream?

   Yes, _____ does.

7. Do you _____ _____ ice cream?

   Yes, I _____.

8. Does he _____ _____ ice cream?

   No, _____ _____.

Section G — Let's have fun

At the ice cream shop!

don't raspberry do like you flavor she does

1. Which _____ do you like? I _____ chocolate flavor.

2. Which flavor _____ you like? I like _____ flavor.

3. Which flavor _____ she like? _____ likes mint flavor.

4. Do _____ like vanilla flavor? No, I _____.

Do or Does?

1. What flavor _____ she like?

2. What flavor _____ they like?

3. What flavor _____ he like?

4. What flavor _____ you like?

5. _____ you like strawberry flavor?

6. _____ he like vanilla flavor?

7. _____ they like vanilla flavor?

8. _____ she like vanilla flavor?

9. Yes, they _____.

10. No, she _____ not.

Lesson 15: In the refrigerator

در یخچال

> What do you want to eat?
> I want to eat rice.

Section A — Words

1. rice
برنج
2. salad
سالاد
3. toast
تست
4. soup
سوپ
5. dumplings
دامپلینگ

6. tea
چای
7. cola
کولا
8. eggs
تخم مرغ
9. water
آب
10. ice
یخ

Section B — Make a sentence

What do you want to <u>eat</u>?

I want to eat <u>rice</u>.

I don't want to eat <u>dumplings</u>.

What does he want to <u>drink</u>?

He wants to drink <u>tea</u>.

He doesn't want to drink <u>cola</u>.

| Section C | Make a question |

Do you want to <u>eat</u> <u>salad</u>?

Yes, I do. / No, I don't.

Does she want to <u>drink</u> <u>juice</u>?

Yes, she does. / No, she doesn't.

Alternative: **Yes, she wants to drink juice.**

| Section D | Learn a verb |

sell – selling – sold – sold فروش

They **sell** eggs at the supermarket.

He was **selling** delicious dumplings at the market last night.

Last week, they **sold** me some cheap rice.

The supermarket has never **sold** ice.

| Section E | Learn an idiom |

Be as cold as ice

Meaning: To describe someone who is very unfriendly.

"The teacher *was as cold as ice* after she caught me cheating on the science test."

| Section F | Write |

Trace and fill in the words

1. What _____ you want _____ drink?

I _____ to _____ water.

2. What _____ he want to _____?

He _____ to eat _____.

3. What _____ you want to _____?

I _____ to eat _____.

4. What _____ she _____ to drink?

She wants to _____ _____.

5. _____ you want to _____ toast?

_____, I do.

6. Does _____ want to _____ tea?

No, he _____.

7. Do you _____ to drink _____?

Yes, I _____.

8. Does _____ want to eat _____?

_____, she _____.

Section G Let's have fun

In the refrigerator!

1	2	3	4	5	6	7	8	9	10	11	12	13
a	b	c	d	e	f	g	h	i	j	k	l	m
14	15	16	17	18	19	20	21	22	23	24	25	26
n	o	p	q	r	s	t	u	v	w	x	y	z

Write the words using the code above

1. 19-15-21-16 __ __ __ __
2. 20-15-1-19-20 __ __ __ __ __
3. 19-1-12-1-4 __ __ __ __ __
4. 18-9-3-5 __ __ __ __
5. 23-1-20-5-18 __ __ __ __ __
6. 3-15-12-1 __ __ __ __

This man's refrigerator has no food! Help him write a shopping list!

Shopping list

1. dumplings
2. _____
3. _____
4. _____
5. _____
6. _____
7. _____
8. _____

Lesson 16: Jobs

شغل ها

Section A — Words

1. doctor
دکتر
2. cook
آشپز
3. nurse
پرستار
4. police officer
افسر پلیس
5. taxi driver
راننده تاکسی
6. teacher
معلم
7. farmer
مزرعه دار
8. salesclerk
متصدی فروش
9. firefighter
آتش نشان
10. builder
کارگر ساختمانی

Section B — Make a sentence

What is her job?

She is a <u>doctor</u>.

She isn't a <u>nurse</u>.

What is his job?

He is a <u>teacher</u>.

He isn't a <u>salesclerk</u>.

| Section C | Make a question |

Is he a <u>farmer</u>?

Yes, he is. / No, he isn't.

Are they <u>teacher</u>s?

Yes, they are. / No, they aren't.

Alternative: **Yes, they are teachers.**

| Section D | Learn a verb |

work – working – worked – worked کار کردن

I **work** on a farm every day.

She wasn't **working** at the hospital last year.

My mother **worked** at the police station yesterday.

He hasn't **worked** for two years.

| Section E | Learn an idiom |

Keep up the good work

Meaning: To encourage someone to keep doing well.

"You're doing a great job. *Keep up the good work*."

| Section F | Write |

Trace and fill in the words

1. What is his _____?

He _____ a cook. He isn't a _____.

2. What is _____ job?

She _____ a _____. She _____ a nurse.

3. What _____ his _____?

_____ is a _____. He isn't _____ _____.

4. What is _____ job?

She _____ a _____. She _____ a _____.

5. Is _____ a builder?

No, she _____.

6. _____ they doctors?

No, they _____.

7. Is _____ a _____?

Yes, she _____.

8. Are they _____?

Yes, _____ _____.

Section G — Let's have fun

Jobs!

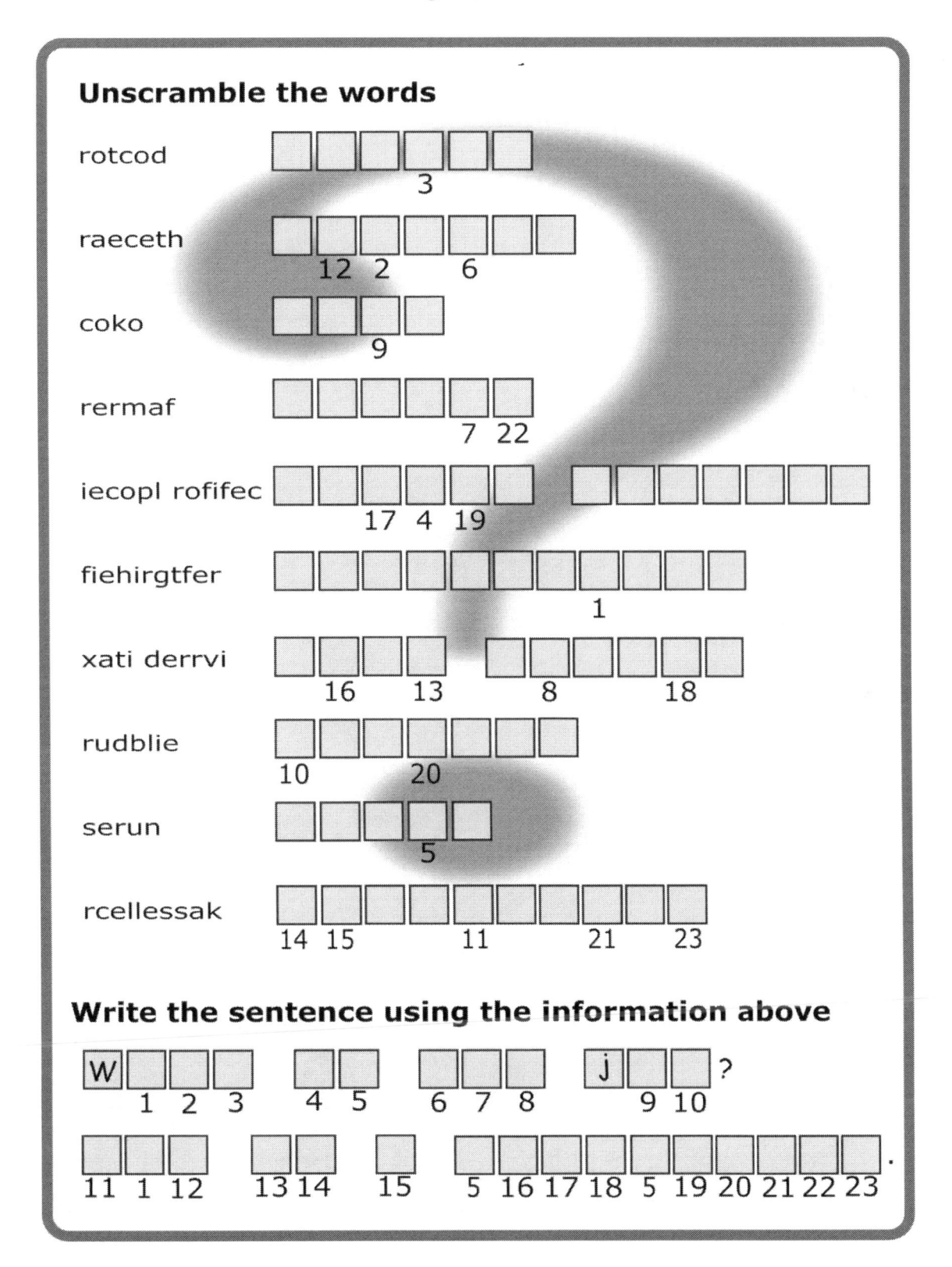

Unscramble the words

rotcod ☐☐☐☐☐☐
           3

raeceth ☐☐☐☐☐☐☐
         12 2   6

coko ☐☐☐☐
       9

rermaf ☐☐☐☐☐☐
          7 22

iecopl rofifec ☐☐☐☐☐☐ ☐☐☐☐☐☐☐
               17 4 19

fiehirgtfer ☐☐☐☐☐☐☐☐☐☐
                  1

xati derrvi ☐☐☐ ☐☐☐☐☐☐
           16 13 8   18

rudblie ☐☐☐☐☐☐☐
        10 20

serun ☐☐☐☐☐
          5

rcellessak ☐☐☐☐☐☐☐☐☐☐
          14 15   11   21 23

Write the sentence using the information above

☐☐☐☐ ☐☐ ☐☐☐☐ ☐☐☐ ?
W 1 2 3   4 5   6 7 8   j 9 10

☐☐☐ ☐☐ ☐ ☐☐☐☐☐☐☐☐☐.
11 1 12 13 14 15 5 16 17 18 5 19 20 21 22 23

Test 4   Lesson 13 - 16

Write the answer next to the letter "A"

A: ___ **1.** What does he want to ___? He ___ to buy some milk.

a. buys, want   b. buy, have   c. buys, wants   d. buy, wants

A: ___ **2.** Do you ___ to buy some ___? Yes, I do.

a. wants, meat   b. want, bread   c. want, apple   d. wants, drinks

A: ___ **3.** She ___ the vegetables at the supermarket.

a. get   b. getting   c. got   d. is get

A: ___ **4.** "That was too expensive. What a rip ___."

a. of   b. over   c. off   d. curl

A: ___ **5.** Which flavor ___ he like? He ___ mint flavor.

a. do, like   b. can, like   c. does, like   d. does, likes

A: ___ **6.** ___ you like chocolate ice cream? Yes, I ___.

a. Does, does   b. Can, does   c. Do, like   d. Do, do

A: ___ **7.** They didn't ___ almond ice cream.

a. have   b. has   c. having   d. had

A: ___ **8.** "That new book is just the ___ of the month."

a. taste   b. word   c. ice cream   d. flavor

A: ___ 9. What ___ she want to drink? She wants to ___ cola.

a. do, try　　　b. does, drink　　　c. can, have　　d. don't, want

A: ___ 10. Do ___ want to eat salad? No, I ___.

a. he, doesn't　b. you, don't　　c. you, not like　　　d. we, haven't

A: ___ 11. They are ___ coffee.

a. sell　　　　b. sells　　　　c. selling　　　d. sold

A: ___ 12. "She wasn't friendly. She was as ___ as ice."

a. melted　　　b. cold　　　　c. dry　　　　d. mean

A: ___ 13. What is ___ job? She ___ a taxi driver.

a. she, is　　　b. hers, can　　　c. she's, be　　d. her, is

A: ___ 14. ___ they teachers? No, they ___.

a. Are, don't　　b. Do, don't　　c. Have, haven't　　d. Are, aren't

A: ___ 15. They ___ at a school.

a. work　　　　b. works　　　　c. working　　　d. has worked

A: ___ 16. "You're doing well. Keep ___ the good work."

a. into　　　　b. on　　　　c. going　　　d. up

Answers on page 206

Lesson 17: Names

نام ها

What's her name?
Her name is Helen.

Section A — Words

1. John
جان
2. Matthew
متی
3. Jason
جیسون
4. Helen
هلن
5. Mary
مریم
6. Kevin
کوین
7. Tom
تام
8. Emily
امیلی
9. Jessica
جسیکا
10. Susan
سوزان

Section B — Make a sentence

What's **your** name?

My name is **John**.

My name isn't **Jason**.

What's **her** name?

Her name is **Susan**.

Her name isn't **Mary**.

Note: What's = What is

Section C — Make a question

Is his name Jason?

Yes, it is. / No, it isn't.

Is her name Emily?

Yes, it is. / No, it isn't.

Alternative: **Yes, her name is Emily.**

Section D — Learn a verb

call – calling – called – called صدا کردن, تماس گرفتن

You can **call** him Jason.

I will be **calling** you tomorrow at 9:30 A.M.

Kevin **called** Mary yesterday.

Helen hasn't **called** Matthew back yet.

Section E — Learn an idiom

A household name

Meaning: To describe someone famous who everyone knows.

"The actor became *a household name* after he won an Oscar for his performance."

| Section F | Write |

Trace and fill in the words

1. What's _____ name?

   _____ name _____ Susan. Her name isn't _____.

2. What's his _____?

   His name _____ _____. His name _____ John.

3. _____ _____ name?

   My _____ is _____. My name _____ _____.

4. What's _____ _____?

   Her name _____ _____. Her _____ isn't Mary.

5. Is _____ name _____?

   Yes, _____ is.

6. _____ her _____ Jessica?

   No, it _____.

7. Is _____ name _____?

   Yes, it _____.

8. Is _____ _____ Kevin?

   No, _____ _____.

Section G | Let's have fun

Names!

1	2	3	4	5
M	T	S	J	K

Write their names

1. __ __ __ __

2. __ __ __

3. __ __ __ __ __

4. __ __ __ __

5. __ __ __ __ __ __

What's your name?

_____

Answer the questions

1. What is her name?

   Her name is Mary.

2. What is his name?

   _____

3. What is her name?

   _____

4. What is his name?

   _____

5. What is his name?

   _____

Lesson 18: More places

مکانهای بیشتر

Where did you go yesterday?
I went to school.

Section A — Words

1. the library
كتابخانه
2. school
مدرسه
3. the hospital
بیمارستان
4. the train station
ایستگاه قطار
5. the police station
ایستگاه پلیس
6. the office
دفتر
7. the factory
کارخانه
8. the clinic
درمانگاه
9. the bus stop
ایستگاه اتوبوس
10. the fire station
ایستگاه آتشنشانی

Section B — Make a sentence

Where did you go <u>yesterday</u>?

I went to <u>the library</u>.

I didn't go to <u>the clinic</u>.

Where did they go <u>last week</u>?

They went to <u>the office</u>.

They didn't go to <u>the police station</u>.

Learn: yesterday, last week, last night, last month

Note: didn't = did not

Section C — Make a question

Did she go to <u>school</u> <u>last night</u>?
Yes, she did. / No, she didn't.

Did you go to <u>the factory</u> <u>yesterday</u>?
Yes, I did. / No, I didn't.

Alternative: **Yes, I went there.**

Section D — Learn a verb

go – going – went – gone رفتن

I will **go** to the library after school.

When I was **going** to the office, I saw my friend.

Matthew **went** to the clinic this morning.

Mary hasn't **gone** to school yet.

Section E — Learn an idiom

Heart is in the right place

Meaning: To mean well and try to do the right thing.

"He makes a lot of mistakes, but his *heart is in the right place*."

| Section F | Write |

Trace and fill in the words

1. _____ did you _____ yesterday?

   I _____ to the police _____.

2. Where _____ they go _____ night?

   _____ went to _____ clinic.

3. Where _____ you _____ last week?

   _____ went to the _____.

4. Where did _____ go _____?

   She _____ to the _____.

5. Did he go _____ the bus _____ yesterday?

   Yes, he _____.

6. Did you _____ to the train _____ last _____?

   No, I _____.

7. Did _____ go to the _____ last week?

   Yes, _____ _____.

8. Did she _____ to the _____ last night?

   No, _____ _____.

Section G Let's have fun

More places!

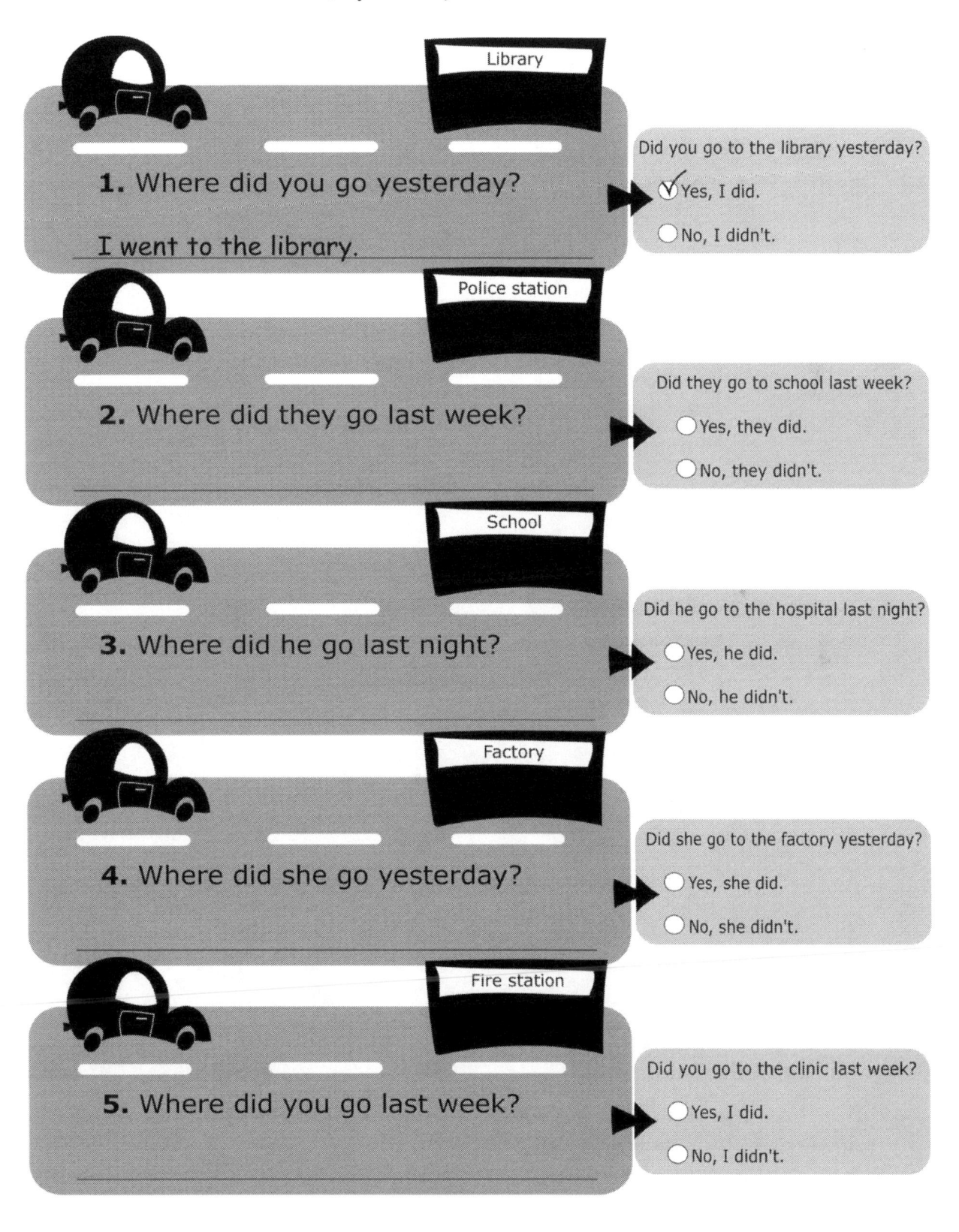

Library

1. Where did you go yesterday?

I went to the library.

Did you go to the library yesterday?
- ✓ Yes, I did.
- ○ No, I didn't.

Police station

2. Where did they go last week?

Did they go to school last week?
- ○ Yes, they did.
- ○ No, they didn't.

School

3. Where did he go last night?

Did he go to the hospital last night?
- ○ Yes, he did.
- ○ No, he didn't.

Factory

4. Where did she go yesterday?

Did she go to the factory yesterday?
- ○ Yes, she did.
- ○ No, she didn't.

Fire station

5. Where did you go last week?

Did you go to the clinic last week?
- ○ Yes, I did.
- ○ No, I didn't.

Lesson 19: Meats

گوشت

What did he eat for lunch?
He ate chicken.

Section A — Words

1. **beef**
گوشت گاو
2. **pork**
گوشت خوک
3. **bacon**
بیکن
4. **fish**
ماهی
5. **salami**
سالامی
6. **chicken**
جوجه
7. **lamb**
گوشت بره
8. **ham**
ژامبون
9. **sausage**
سوسیس
10. **shrimp**
میگو

Section B — Make a sentence

What did he eat for <u>lunch</u>?

He ate <u>beef</u>.

He didn't eat <u>chicken</u>.

What did you eat for <u>dinner</u>?

We ate <u>lamb</u>.

We didn't eat <u>pork</u>.

Learn: breakfast, lunch, dinner

Section C — Make a question

Did they eat <u>ham</u> for <u>breakfast</u>?
Yes, they did. / No, they didn't.

Did you eat <u>fish</u> for <u>dinner</u>?
Yes, I did. / No, I didn't.

Alternative: **Yes, we ate fish.**

Section D — Learn a verb

eat – eating – ate – eaten خوردن

I **eat** bacon for breakfast every Sunday.

They're not **eating** meat.

We **ate** a sandwich with cheese and salami yesterday.

I had never **eaten** German sausages until I went there.

Section E — Learn an idiom

Beef up

Meaning: To strengthen something or somebody.

"We need to *beef up* our efforts if we are going to do well this year."

Section F — Write

Trace and fill in the words

1. What _____ she eat _____ lunch?

She ate _____. She _____ eat fish.

2. What did _____ eat for _____?

They _____ pork. They didn't _____ shrimp.

3. What _____ he eat _____ lunch?

_____ ate _____. He didn't _____ beef.

4. _____ did you _____ for breakfast?

I _____ fish. _____ didn't eat _____.

5. _____ you eat _____ for lunch?

Yes, we _____.

6. Did _____ eat _____ _____ dinner?

No, I _____.

7. Did _____ eat _____ for _____?

Yes, he _____.

8. _____ they _____ bacon for _____?

No, _____ _____.

Section G | Let's have fun

Meats!

Find the words!

```
f e p l x e m s x h e m d b o h z a l u
e p r n y l o q u y m x y r w g r p g d
i c r l y o i q d z m a u a p f q b s g
r v b k v y b n e z i x x q d r e c b h
r y u o r w l j g d s n z u u s l l z z
l h b e e f k w v q n b j e g f b w c m
c i b k b s q x b g m o i g n k n d r p
f q x b q a e k m f j o c b l s p k h n
m x j t o u n z z m f f s a l a m i y y
v i r m i a k e s k r g e k b u m z a e
w n p w n k q z r v h p h e s s n b l p
q o h n s t q u c n w u z l r a d f u v
a p s i g e l b o b q f x w s g n d e w
l b k p j c g n n c x o i z q e t e r i
s g n s x v w q l o x h k y k b q q y y
j k a x e h x a s z y p a c k r e v t r
j o w n g q v f i s h r i m p n o f m p
o a d h o b i e t h o h c q z n c p b m
y k o b m l v h v i c r q i k b c o f i
f i q a m x g l q k z w s n a w t n w w
```

~~beef~~   shrimp
pork   bacon
ham   sausage
fish   lamb
chicken salami

Lesson 20: Vegetables

سبزیجات

> What will you cook tonight?
> I will cook pumpkin.

Section A — Words

1. **pumpkin**
   كدو حلوايي
2. **potato**
   سیب زمینی
3. **carrot**
   هویج
4. **asparagus**
   مارچوبه
5. **broccoli**
   کلم بروکلی
6. **corn**
   ذرت
7. **cabbage**
   کلم
8. **spinach**
   اسفناج
9. **mushroom**
   قارچ
10. **onion**
    پیاز

Section B — Make a sentence

What will he cook <u>tonight</u>?

He will cook <u>pumpkin</u>.

He won't cook <u>spinach</u>.

What won't she cook <u>tomorrow</u>?

She won't cook <u>onion</u>.

She will cook <u>carrot</u>.

Learn: tonight, tomorrow, later, next week

Note: won't = will not

Section C — Make a question

Will we cook <u>carrot</u> <u>later</u>?

Yes, we will. / No, we won't.

Will you cook <u>asparagus</u> <u>tomorrow</u>?

Yes, I will. / No, I won't.

Alternative: **Yes, I will cook asparagus.**

Section D — Learn a verb

cook – cooking – cooked – cooked پختن

She always **cooks** onions with the potatoes.

Mary will be **cooking** dinner for us tonight.

John **cooked** a delicious meal for us last weekend.

I've **cooked** cabbage and mushroom a lot lately.

Section E — Learn an idiom

Carrot on a stick

Meaning: A reward that is promised upon completion of a task.

"The coach gave his players a *carrot on a stick* and promised to take them all out for dinner if they win the game."

Section F | Write

Trace and fill in the words

1. What _____ he cook _____?

He will _____ corn. He _____ cook _____.

2. What _____ she _____ tomorrow?

She won't _____ spinach. She will cook _____.

3. What _____ he _____ later?

_____ will _____ onion. He won't cook _____.

4. What will _____ cook tonight?

She _____ cook _____. She _____ cook onion.

5. Will _____ cook _____ tomorrow?

Yes, they _____.

6. Will you _____ asparagus _____?

No, I _____.

7. Will she _____ mushroom _____?

Yes, _____ will.

8. Will _____ cook _____ tomorrow?

No, we _____.

94

Section G | Let's have fun

Vegetables!

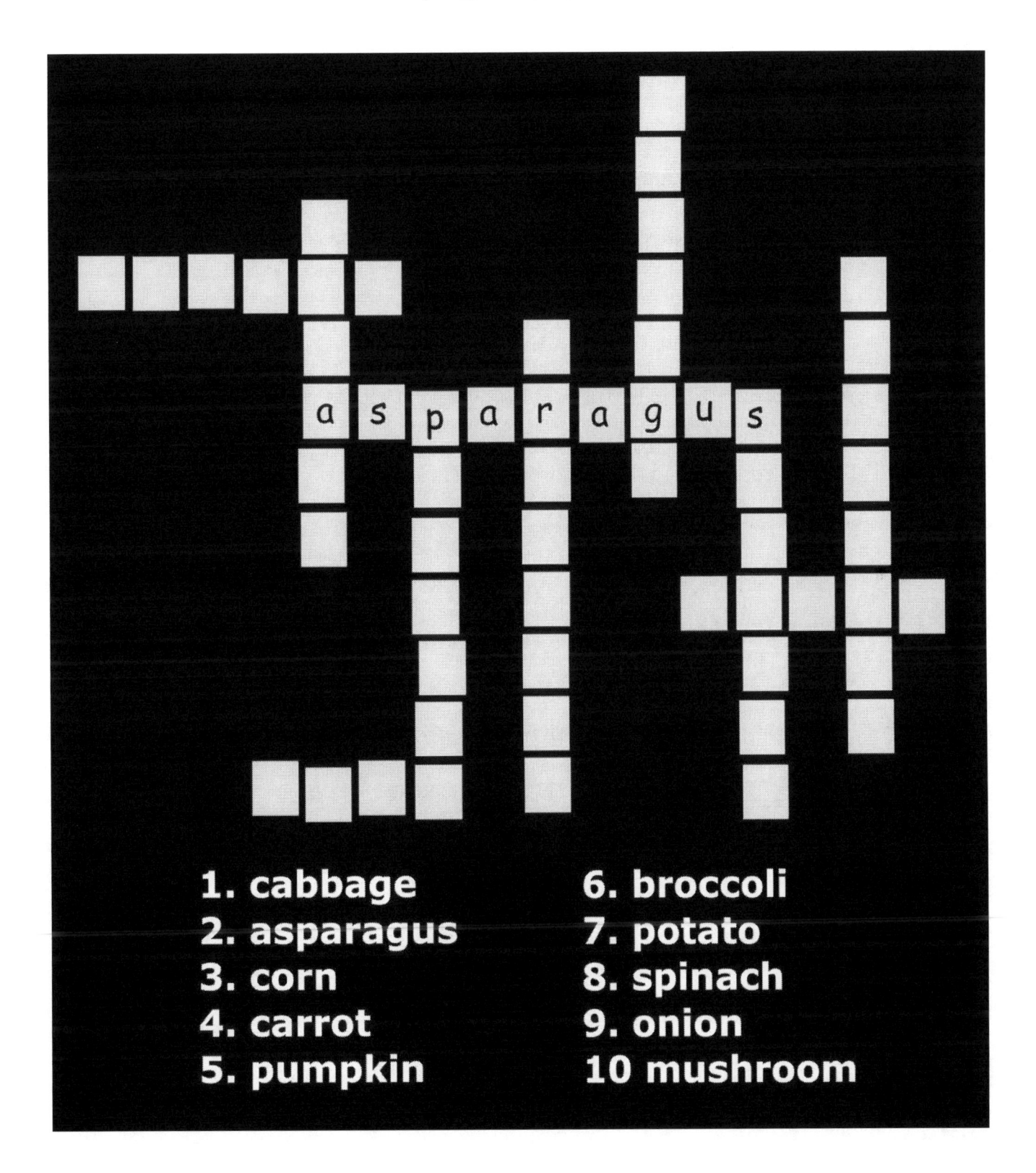

a s p a r a g u s

1. cabbage
2. asparagus
3. corn
4. carrot
5. pumpkin
6. broccoli
7. potato
8. spinach
9. onion
10 mushroom

Test 5   Lesson 17 - 20

Write the answer next to the letter "A"

A: ___ **1.** What's her ___? ___ name is Helen.

a. name, Her   b. name, She's   c. names, Her   d. name, She

A: ___ **2.** ___ his name Kevin? Yes, ___ is.

a. Is, it   b. Is, he   c. Can, it   d. Does, it

A: ___ **3.** Yesterday, Matthew ___ a green marker.

a. has   b. is having   c. had   d. did had

A: ___ **4.** "She's really famous. She's a ___ name."

a. homely   b. household   c. real   d. star

A: ___ **5.** Where ___ you go yesterday? I ___ to the clinic.

a. do, go   b. did, go   c. does, went   d. did, went

A: ___ **6.** ___ she go to the office last night? Yes, she ___.

a. Does, go   b. Can, does   c. Did, goes   d. Did, did

A: ___ **7.** I ___ to the train station every week.

a. gone   b. go   c. going   d. goes

A: ___ **8.** "He means well. His ___ is in the right place."

a. heart   b. words   c. mind   d. smile

A: ___ **9.** What ___ he eat for dinner? He ___ eat pork.

a. does, didn't b. is, is c. didn't, didn't d. did, was

A: ___ **10.** ___ they eat sausage for lunch? No, they ___.

a. Were, weren't b. Did, don't c. Like, not like d. Did, didn't

A: ___ **11.** She has ___ all of the ham.

a. eat b. ate c. eaten d. eating

A: ___ **12.** "He wants to get stronger. He said he wants to beef ___."

a. out b. up c. on d. in

A: ___ **13.** What ___ he cook later? He will ___ broccoli.

a. is, cook b. will, cooks c. has, cook d. will, cook

A: ___ **14.** ___ we cook asparagus tonight? ___, we will.

a. Can, Can b. Don't, Do c. Will, Yes d. Are, Yes

A: ___ **15.** She will ___ vegetables tomorrow.

a. cook b. cooks c. cooking d. cooked

A: ___ **16.** "I think the reward is like a ___ on a stick."

a. potato b. pumpkin c. carrot d. mushroom

Answers on page 206

Lesson 21: At school

در مدرسه

> Where is the art room?
> The art room is next to the gym.

Section A — Words

1. **classroom**
   کلاس درس
2. **office**
   دفتر
3. **nurse's office**
   دفتر پرستاران
4. **gym**
   سالن ورزش
5. **hall**
   سالن
6. **computer lab**
   آزمایشگاه کامپیوتر
7. **art room**
   اتاق هنر
8. **music room**
   اتاق موسیقی
9. **science lab**
   آزمایشگاه علوم
10. **lunchroom**
    اتاق ناهار خوری

Section B — Make a sentence

Where is the <u>classroom</u>?

The classroom is <u>across from</u> the <u>office</u>.

The classroom isn't <u>next to</u> the <u>science lab</u>.

Where is the <u>computer lab</u>?

The computer lab is <u>between</u> the <u>gym</u> and the <u>hall</u>.

The computer lab isn't <u>across from</u> the <u>art room</u>.

Learn: across from, next to, between

Section C — Make a question

Is the <u>art room</u> <u>next to</u> the <u>music room</u>?

Yes, it is. / No, it's <u>next to</u> the <u>science lab</u>.

Is the <u>nurse's office</u> <u>next to</u> the <u>office</u>?

Yes, it is. / No, it's <u>across from</u> the <u>computer lab</u>.

Alternative: **Yes, it's next to the office.**

Section D — Learn a verb

put – putting – put – put قرار دادن, گذاشتن

You can **put** the guitar in the music room.

We are **putting** the chairs in the new office.

The students already **put** the books in the computer lab.

She hasn't **put** any food in the lunchroom yet.

Section E — Learn an idiom

Old school

Meaning: To do something the old-fashioned way.

"We're going to do this *old school* and use a hammer and nails."

Section F Write

Trace and fill in the words

1. Where _____ the _____?

   The office is next _____ the _____.

2. Where _____ the gym?

   The gym is _____ the art _____ and the science lab.

3. Where _____ the _____ room?

   The music room is _____ from the _____.

4. _____ is the _____ lab?

   The science lab is _____ the lunchroom and the _____.

5. Is the art _____ next to the _____ room?

   Yes, _____ is.

6. Is the _____ lab _____ to the hall?

   No, it's _____ the gym _____ the art _____.

7. _____ the nurse's _____ next to the _____?

   Yes, _____ _____.

8. Is _____ hall across _____ the classroom?

   No, it's _____ the _____ and _____ office.

100

Section G Let's have fun

At school!

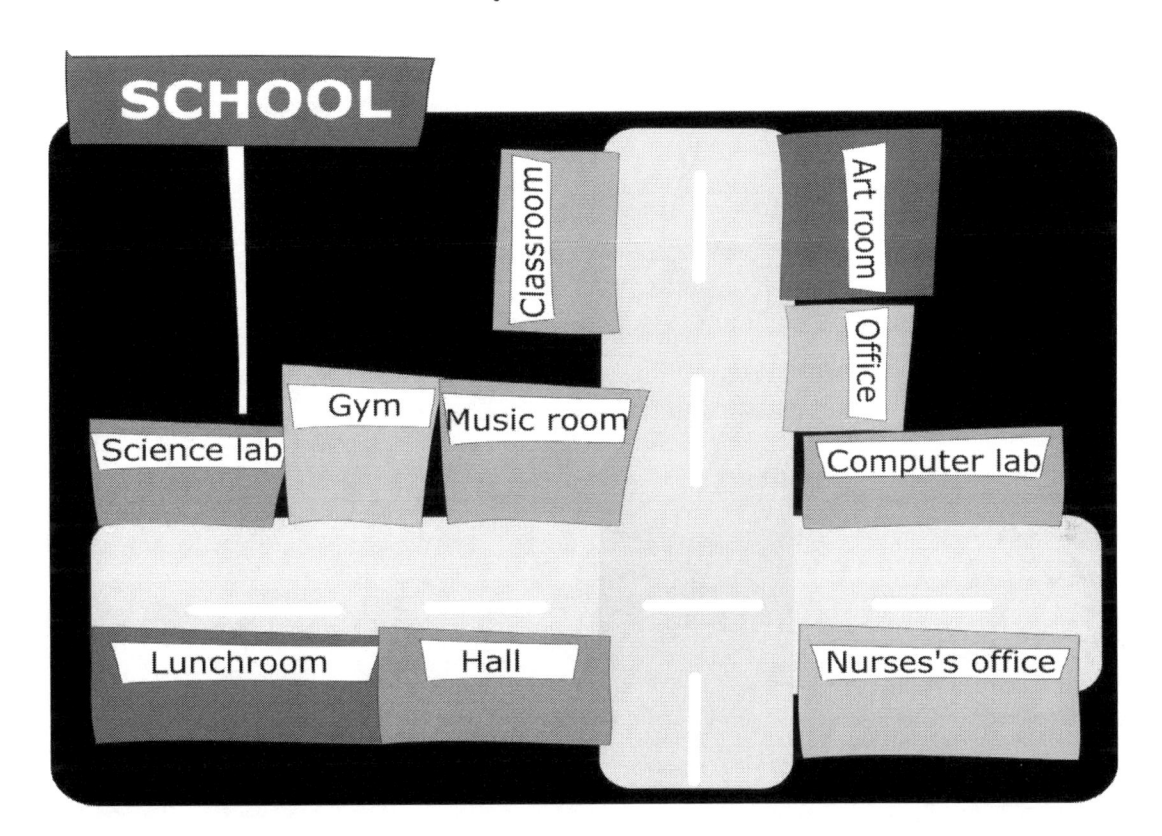

Answer the questions

1. Where is the gym?
   _____.

2. Where is the classroom?
   _____.

3. Where is the nurse's office?
   _____.

4. Is the lunchroom next to the hall?
   _____.

5. Is the science lab across from the office?
   _____.

Lesson 22: School subjects

موضوعات مدرسه

What class do you have after math?
I have an art class after math.

Section A — Words

1. science
   علوم پایه
2. English
   انگلیسی
3. P.E.
   ورزش (تربیت بدنی)
4. geography
   جغرافیا
5. social studies
   تعلیمات اجتماعی
6. math
   ریاضی
7. art
   هنر
8. music
   موسیقی
9. history
   تاریخ
10. computer
    کامپیوتر

Section B — Make a sentence

What class do you have <u>after</u> <u>science</u>?

I have a <u>geography</u> class after science.

I don't have a <u>computer</u> class after science.

What class does he have <u>before</u> <u>math</u>?

He has a <u>history</u> class before math.

He doesn't have an <u>English</u> class before math.

Learn: after, before / have, has

Section C — Make a question

Do you have a <u>math</u> class after <u>history</u>?

Yes, I do. / No, I have a <u>music</u> class.

Does he have a <u>math</u> class before <u>English</u>?

Yes, he does. / No, he has a <u>computer</u> class.

Alternative: **Yes, he has a math class.**

Section D — Learn a verb

do – doing – did – done انجام دادن

He couldn't **do** most of the questions on the math test.

They are **doing** the science project now.

John **did** really well on his English test last semester.

I will have already **done** the history homework by Sunday.

Section E — Learn an idiom

Cut class

Meaning: To miss class on purpose.

"Jenny *cut class* after she realized she didn't do her math homework."

Section F   Write

Trace and fill in the words

1. What class _____ you have _____ math?

I have _____ English class after _____.

2. What class _____ she _____ before art?

She _____ a music _____ before art.

3. What _____ do you have _____ history?

I _____ a geography class before _____.

4. What class does _____ have after _____?

She _____ a science class _____ P.E.

5. Do you _____ a math class after history?

Yes, I _____.

6. Does he have a science _____ after _____?

No, he _____ a computer _____.

7. Do _____ have _____ art class before _____?

Yes, I _____.

8. Does _____ have a P.E. class _____ music?

No, she _____ an _____ class.

Section G   Let's have fun

School Subjects!

I have a geography class after science.
I have an English class before science.
I have a math class before English.
I have a history class after geography.
I have a computer class before math.

Fill out the School Schedule using the information above

School Schedule

9am   _____

10am   _____

11am   _____

1pm   ___science class___

2pm   _____

3pm   _____

True or False? Circle the answer

1. You have a science class before geography.   **True   False**

2. You have a computer class after math.   **True   False**

3. You have a history class after geography.   **True   False**

4. You have an English class after science.   **True   False**

Lesson 23: Chores

کارها

What do you need to do today?
I need to feed the pets.

Section A | Words

1. **wash the dishes**
   شستن ظرف ها
2. **feed the pets**
   خوراک دادن به حیوانات خانگی
3. **vacuum the carpet**
   فرش را جارو کن
4. **take out the trash**
   بیرون گذاشتن آشغال
5. **clean the bedroom**
   تمیز کردن اتاق خواب
6. **mop the floor**
   تمیز کردن زمین
7. **cook dinner**
   شام پختن
8. **do the laundry**
   شستن لباس ها
9. **iron the clothes**
   اتو کردن لباس ها
10. **make the beds**
    مرتب کردن تخت ها

Section B | Make a sentence

What do you need to do <u>this morning</u>?

This morning, I need to <u>wash the dishes</u>.

This morning, I don't need to <u>make the beds</u>.

What does he need to do <u>this afternoon</u>?

This afternoon, he needs to <u>mop the floor</u>.

This evening, he doesn't need to <u>clean the bedroom</u>.

Learn: this morning, this afternoon, this evening, today

Section C — Make a question

Do you need to make the beds this morning?
Yes, I do. / No, I don't.

Does he need to iron the clothes this afternoon?
Yes, he does. / No, he doesn't.

Alternative: **Yes, he needs to iron the clothes.**

Section D — Learn a verb

know – knowing – knew – known دانستن

I don't **know** what to feed the pets.

There is no way of **knowing** which chores have been done.

Mary **knew** the trash hadn't been taken out yet.

I hadn't **known** at the time that nobody did the laundry.

Section E — Learn an idiom

All in a day's work

Meaning: A normal day without a change in routine.

"Taking out the trash before school is *all in a day's work*."

Section F **Write**

Trace and fill in the words

1. _____ do you _____ to do this _____?

_____ afternoon, I need to _____ the laundry.

2. What _____ he _____ to do this _____?

_____ morning, he _____ to _____ the beds.

3. _____ do you need _____ do this _____?

This afternoon, _____ need to feed the _____.

4. What _____ she _____ to _____ today?

Today, _____ needs _____ do the _____.

5. _____ you need to iron the _____ this evening?

Yes, I _____.

6. Does he need to _____ the beds this _____?

No, _____ _____.

7. Do _____ need to _____ the carpet _____?

No, I _____.

8. _____ she need to cook _____ this _____?

Yes, she _____ to _____ dinner.

Section G | Let's have fun

Chores!

Connect the sentences

What do you need to do this morning? • — • This morning, she needs to do the dishes.

What does he need to do this afternoon? • — • This morning, I need to wash the clothes.

What does she need to do this morning? • • This evening, they need to cook dinner.

What do they need to do this evening? • • This afternoon, we need to make the beds.

What do we need to do this afternoon? • • This afternoon, he needs to feed the pets.

Unscramble the sentences

wash the / morning / need to / I / this / dishes

1. _____.

she / the pets / needs to / this afternoon / feed

2. _____.

to / the laundry / need / they / do / this evening

3. _____.

this afternoon / the trash / he / needs to / take out

4. _____.

Lesson 24: At the toy store

در فروشگاه اسباب بازی

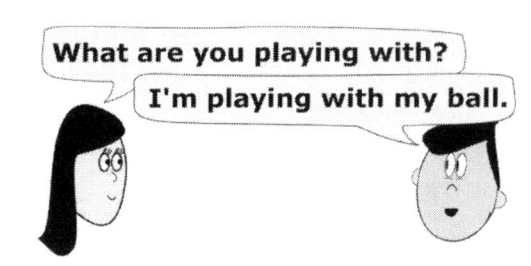

> What are you playing with?
> I'm playing with my ball.

Section A — Words

1. doll
عروسک
2. teddy bear
خرس عروسکی
3. car
ماشین
4. airplane
هواپیما
5. dinosaur
دایناسور
6. robot
ربات-آدم آهنی
7. ball
توپ
8. jump rope
طناب بازی
9. board game
صفحه ی بازی
10. blocks
بلوک ها

Section B — Make a sentence

What are you playing with?

I am playing with <u>my doll</u>.

I am not playing with <u>my dinosaur</u>.

What is he playing with?

He is playing with <u>his robot</u>.

He isn't playing with <u>his blocks</u>.

Learn: my, your, his, her, their, our, its

| Section C | Make a question |

Are you playing with <u>your</u> <u>teddy bear</u>?
Yes, I am. / No, I'm not.

Is she playing with <u>her</u> <u>ball</u>?
Yes, she is. / No, she isn't.

Alternative: **Yes, she is playing with her ball.**

| Section D | Learn a verb |

borrow – borrowing – borrowed – borrowed قرض گرفتن

You can **borrow** my ball.

She will be **borrowing** the board game for tonight.

I **borrowed** a book about cars from the library yesterday.

They haven't **borrowed** these books yet.

| Section E | Learn an idiom |

Like a kid with a new toy

Meaning: To be really happy with something.

"He was *like a kid with a new toy* when he drove the car for the first time."

| Section F | Write |

Trace and fill in the words

1. What _____ you _____ with?

I _____ playing _____ my teddy _____.

2. _____ is _____ playing _____?

She _____ playing with _____ _____.

3. What _____ _____ playing _____?

We _____ _____ with _____ board _____.

4. _____ is he _____ _____?

_____ is _____ with his _____.

5. _____ you playing _____ _____ car?

Yes, I _____ playing _____ my _____.

6. _____ he _____ with _____ airplane?

_____, _____ isn't.

7. _____ you _____ with your _____ rope?

_____, I'm _____.

8. _____ she playing _____ _____ dinosaur?

Yes, _____ _____.

Section G | Let's have fun

Toys!

Circle the toys

1. cool   geography   bag   (doll)   sister

2. desk   blocks   math   father   milk

3. teddy bear   history   classroom   beef

4. pen   science   water   ball   gym

Write the word

1.
2.
3.
4.

Write the answer using the information above

1. What is she playing with? _____.

2. What is he playing with? _____.

3. Is she playing with her teddy bear? _____.

4. Is he playing with his robot? _____.

Test 6   Lesson 21 - 24

Write the answer next to the letter "A"

A: ___ **1.** ___ is the office? It's ___ to the gym.

a. There, next   b. Where, next   c. How, near   d. This, next

A: ___ **2.** ___ the hall across from the office? Yes, ___ is.

a. Does, it   b. Is, it   c. Are, they   d. Can, he

A: ___ **3.** They will ___ the art room later.

a. find   b. found   c. finding   d. finds

A: ___ **4.** "We did it the old-fashioned way. We did it old ___."

a. way   b. time   c. man   d. school

A: ___ **5.** What class ___ you ___ after science?

a. are, have   b. does, has   c. do, have   d. can, has

A: ___ **6.** ___ we have math class after art? Yes, we ___.

a. Can, are   b. Does, do   c. Do, do   d. Are, are

A: ___ **7.** They ___ gym class earlier today.

a. has   b. having   c. are had   d. had

A: ___ **8.** "She ___ class because she didn't do her homework."

a. put   b. cut   c. lost   d. made

A: ___ **9.** This morning, I ___ to ___ the pets.

a. need, feedb. am, takec. can, walkd. need, make

A: ___ **10.** ___ we need to ___ the beds this morning?

a. Does, takeb. Are, openc. Do, mopd. Do, make

A: ___ **11.** He ___ to do the laundry before lunch.

a. needsb. needc. needingd. is need

A: ___ **12.** "Cleaning the room after school is all in a day's ___."

a. timeb. workc. traveld. test

A: ___ **13.** What are you ___ with? I'm playing ___ my robot.

a. play, withb. playing, withc. plays, byd. play, on

A: ___ **14.** Is he playing with ___ jump rope? Yes, he ___.

a. him, canb. he, isc. his, isd. him, has

A: ___ **15.** She doesn't like to ___ with dinosaurs.

a. playsb. playingc. playd. played

A: ___ **16.** "He was so happy, he was like a kid with a new ___."

a. carb. bikec. toyd. ball

Answers on page 206

Lesson 25: In the kitchen

در آشپزخانه

> What was he cleaning?
> He was cleaning the stove.

Section A — Words

1. **refrigerator**
   یخچال
2. **coffee maker**
   قهوه ساز
3. **microwave oven**
   اجاق مایکروویو
4. **stove**
   اجاق گاز
5. **blender**
   مخلوط کن
6. **cupboard**
   کابینت
7. **rice cooker**
   پلوپز
8. **dish rack**
   قفسه ظرف
9. **pan**
   ماهی تابه
10. **toaster**
    توستر

Section B — Make a sentence

What was he cleaning?

He was cleaning the <u>refrigerator</u>.

He wasn't cleaning the <u>stove</u>.

What were they cleaning?

They were cleaning the <u>cupboard</u>.

They weren't cleaning the <u>rice cooker</u>.

Note: weren't = were not, wasn't = was not

Section C — Make a question

Was she cleaning the <u>coffee maker</u>?
Yes, she was. / No, she wasn't.

Were they cleaning the <u>toaster</u>?
Yes, they were. / No, they weren't.

Alternative: **Yes, they were cleaning the toaster.**

Section D — Learn a verb

clean – cleaning – cleaned – cleaned تمیزکردن

He **cleans** the gas stove every day.

We are **cleaning** the refrigerator.

My mother **cleaned** the toaster this morning.

I've already **cleaned** the blender, so you can use it now.

Section E — Learn an idiom

Too many cooks in the kitchen

Meaning: When too many people try to take control.

"We couldn't find a solution because there were *too many cooks in the kitchen*."

| Section F | Write |

Trace and fill in the words

1. What _____ _____ cleaning?

   She _____ _____ _____ cupboard.

2. _____ were _____ cleaning?

   They _____ _____ the _____ maker.

3. What _____ he _____?

   _____ wasn't _____ _____ pan.

4. _____ were _____ cleaning?

   They _____ cleaning _____ _____.

5. Was _____ cleaning _____ microwave _____?

   _____, _____ wasn't.

6. _____ we _____ _____ stove?

   No, _____ _____.

7. Was _____ cleaning the _____?

   Yes, she _____ _____ the refrigerator.

8. _____ they _____ the blender?

   Yes, _____ were _____ the _____.

Section G — Let's have fun

In the kitchen!

Write the missing words

| wasn't | was | you | were | pan | cleaning | she | the |

1. What _____ he cleaning? He was _____ the microwave.

2. What _____ they cleaning? They were cleaning _____ stove.

3. What was _____ cleaning? She was cleaning the _____.

4. Were _____ cleaning the blender? No, I _____.

Was or Were?

1. What _____ she cleaning?

She _____ cleaning the blender.

2. What _____ they cleaning?

They _____ cleaning the toaster.

3. What _____ you cleaning?

I _____ cleaning the refrigerator.

4. _____ he cleaning the cupboard?

Yes, he _____.

5. _____ they cleaning the rice cooker?

No, they _____ not.

Lesson 26: In the toolbox

در جعبه ابزار

What were you using to fix the chair?
I was using the electric drill.

Section A — Words

1. **hammer**
   چکش
2. **electric drill**
   مته برقی
3. **screwdriver**
   پیچ گوشتی
4. **paintbrush**
   قلم مو
5. **shovel**
   بیل
6. **tape measure**
   نوار اندازه گیری
7. **axe**
   تبر
8. **pliers**
   انبر
9. **ladder**
   نردبان
10. **wrench**
    آچار

Section B — Make a sentence

What were you using to fix the <u>table</u>?

I was using the <u>hammer</u>.

I wasn't using the <u>tape measure</u>.

What was she using to fix the <u>fence</u>?

She was using the <u>pliers</u>.

She wasn't using the <u>wrench</u>.

Learn: table, chair, fence, roof, door, cupboard

Section C — Make a question

Was he using the <u>electric drill</u> to <u>fix the chair</u>?
Yes, he was. / No, he wasn't.

Were they using the <u>ladder</u> to <u>fix the roof</u>?
Yes, they were. / No, they weren't.

Alternative: **Yes, they were using the ladder.**

Section D — Learn a verb

use – using – used – used استفاده کردن

She **uses** the shovel to do the gardening.

They were **using** the wrench last week.

My father **used** the screwdriver earlier today.

My brother has never **used** an electric drill.

Section E — Learn an idiom

Tools of the trade

Meaning: Things that are needed for a specific job.

"My cell phone, diary and calculator are all *tools of the trade*."

Section F — Write

Trace and fill in the words

1. What _____ you _____ to fix _____ table?
   _____ was _____ the _____ drill.

2. _____ was she _____ to _____ the chair?
   _____ _____ using _____ screwdriver.

3. What _____ you _____ to fix _____ door?
   _____ _____ using the _____.

4. What was _____ using to _____ the _____?
   He _____ _____ the ladder.

5. Was _____ using the _____ to fix the cupboard?
   _____, she _____.

6. _____ they _____ the shovel to fix the _____?
   _____, _____ weren't.

7. Was _____ using the _____ to fix the _____?
   _____, he _____.

8. _____ you using _____ hammer to fix the _____?
   Yes, _____ _____.

| Section G | Let's have fun |

In the toolbox!

Was or Were?

He _____ using the electric drill to fix the cupboard.

She _____ using the hammer to fix the fence.

They _____ using the tape measure to fix the door.

We _____ using the ladder to fix the roof.

I _____ using the pliers to fix the table.

John _____ using the screwdriver to fix the chair.

What was fixed?

1. _____   4. _____

2. _____   5. _____

3. _____   6. _____

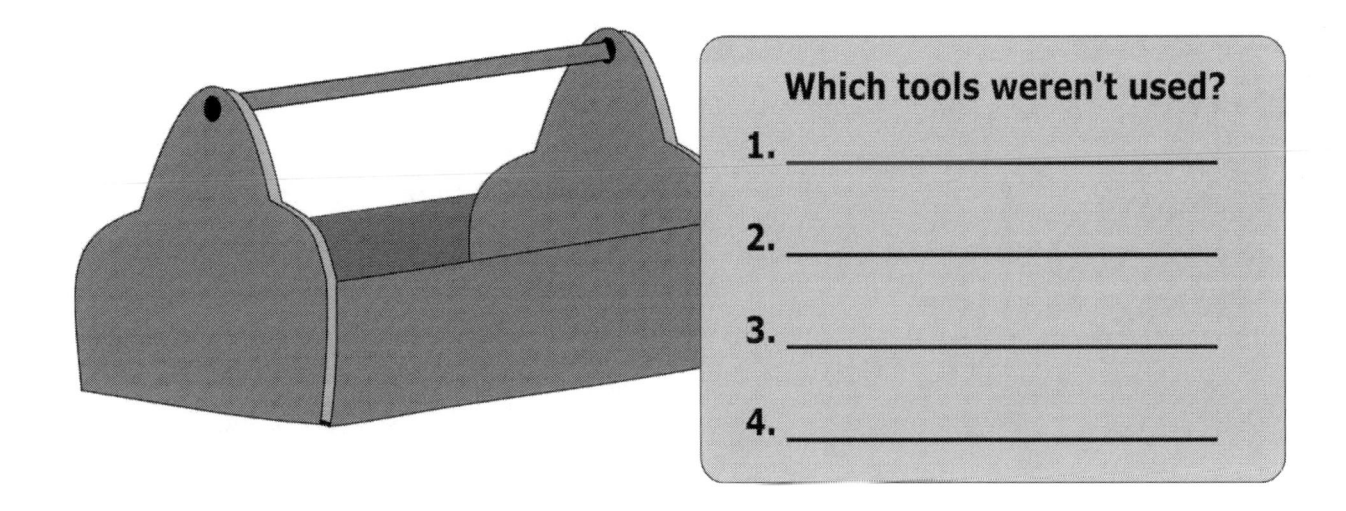

Which tools weren't used?

1. _____

2. _____

3. _____

4. _____

Lesson 27: Transportation

حمل و نقل

> How will you be going to Rome?
> I will be taking a bus.

Section A — Words

1. **catch a bus**
   گرفتن اتوبوس
2. **take a taxi**
   گرفتن تاکسی
3. **take a ferry**
   کرایه ی قایق/کشتی
4. **ride a motorcycle**
   راندن موتورسیکلت
5. **take the subway**
   گرفتن قطار زیر زمینی - مترو
6. **take a train**
   گرفتن قطار
7. **drive a car**
   رانندگی ماشین
8. **ride a scooter**
   راندن اسکوتر (* موتور سیکلت کوچک)
9. **ride a bicycle**
   دوچرخه سواری
10. **take an airplane**
    گرفتن یک هواپیما

Section B — Make a sentence

How will you be going to <u>New York</u>?

I will be <u>catching a bus</u> there.

I won't be <u>riding a scooter</u> there.

Learn: New York, Sydney, Vancouver, Rome, London, Shanghai, Hong Kong, Paris, Berlin, Cape town, Buenos Aires, Venice

Note: I'll = I will

Section C | Make a question

Will you be <u>taking a ferry</u> to <u>Hong Kong</u>?
Yes, I will be. / No, I'll be <u>taking an airplane</u>.

Will you be <u>riding a bicycle</u> to <u>Sydney</u>?
Yes, I will be. / No, I'll be <u>catching a bus</u>.

Alternative: **Yes, I'll be riding a bicycle there.**

Section D | Learn a verb

take – taking – took – taken گرفتن

You can **take** the subway to work.

She will be **taking** a taxi to the restaurant.

We **took** a ferry to the Hong Kong airport last year.

I hadn't **taken** an airplane until I went to Rome.

Section E | Learn an idiom

Lose one's train of thought

Meaning: To forget what you were thinking about.

"I'm sorry, I *lost my train of thought*. What were we talking about?"

Section F — Write

Trace and fill in the words

1. How _____ you be _____ to Sydney?

_____ will be _____ a train _____.

2. _____ will _____ be _____ to Vancouver?

He _____ _____ driving a _____ there.

3. How _____ we _____ going _____ Rome?

_____ will be _____ a scooter _____.

4. _____ will _____ be _____ to Paris?

They _____ be _____ _____ airplane there.

5. Will _____ be _____ a motorcycle _____ Berlin?

No, I'll _____ riding _____ bicycle.

6. Will _____ be _____ a ferry to _____?

No, they'll _____ _____ an airplane.

7. Will _____ be _____ the subway _____ Venice?

No, he'll _____ catching a _____.

8. Will she _____ _____ a train to _____?

Yes, _____ be _____ a _____ there.

126

Section G — Let's have fun

Transportation!

Unscramble the words and write

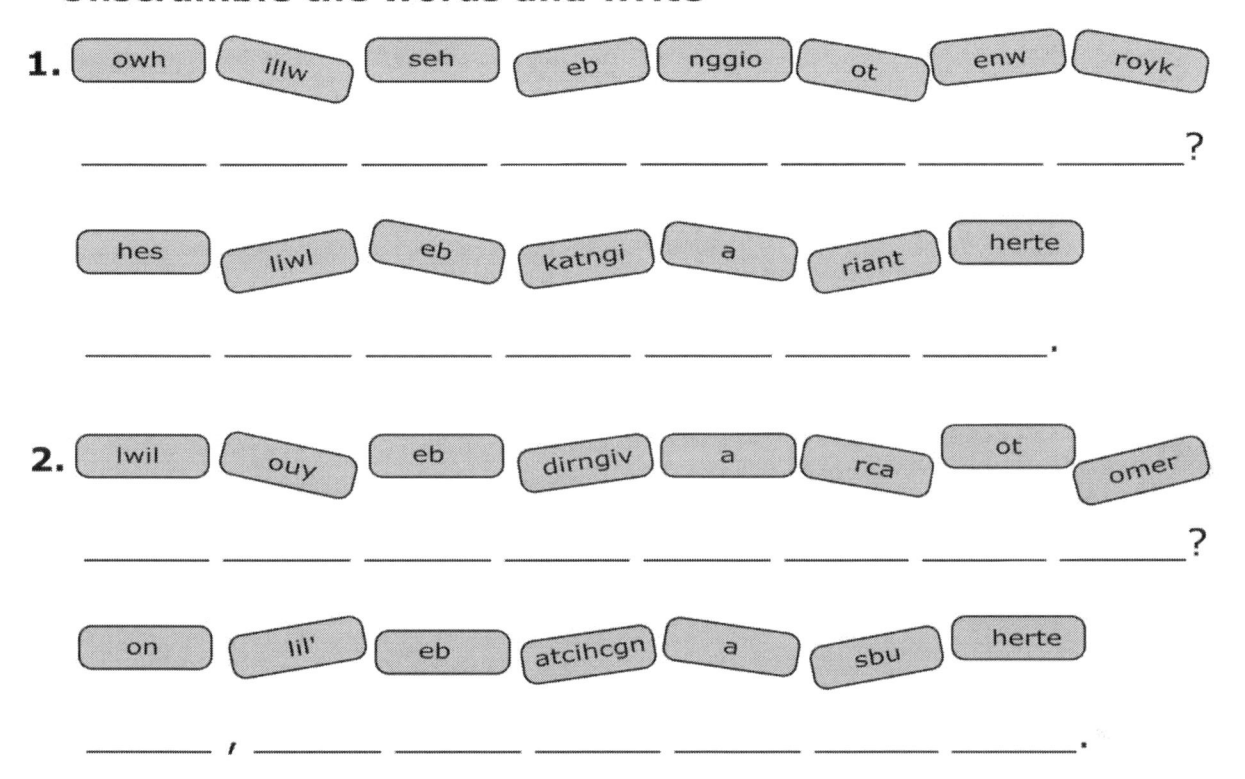

1. owh | illw | seh | eb | nggio | ot | enw | royk

   __How__ __will__ __she__ __be__ __going__ __to__ __New__ __York__?

   hes | liwl | eb | katngi | a | riant | herte

   __She__ __will__ __be__ __taking__ __a__ __train__ __there__.

2. lwil | ouy | eb | dirngiv | a | rca | ot | omer

   __Will__ __you__ __be__ __driving__ __a__ __car__ __to__ __Rome__?

   on | lil' | eb | atcihcgn | a | sbu | herte

   __No__, __I'll__ __be__ __catching__ __a__ __bus__ __there__.

Connect the words

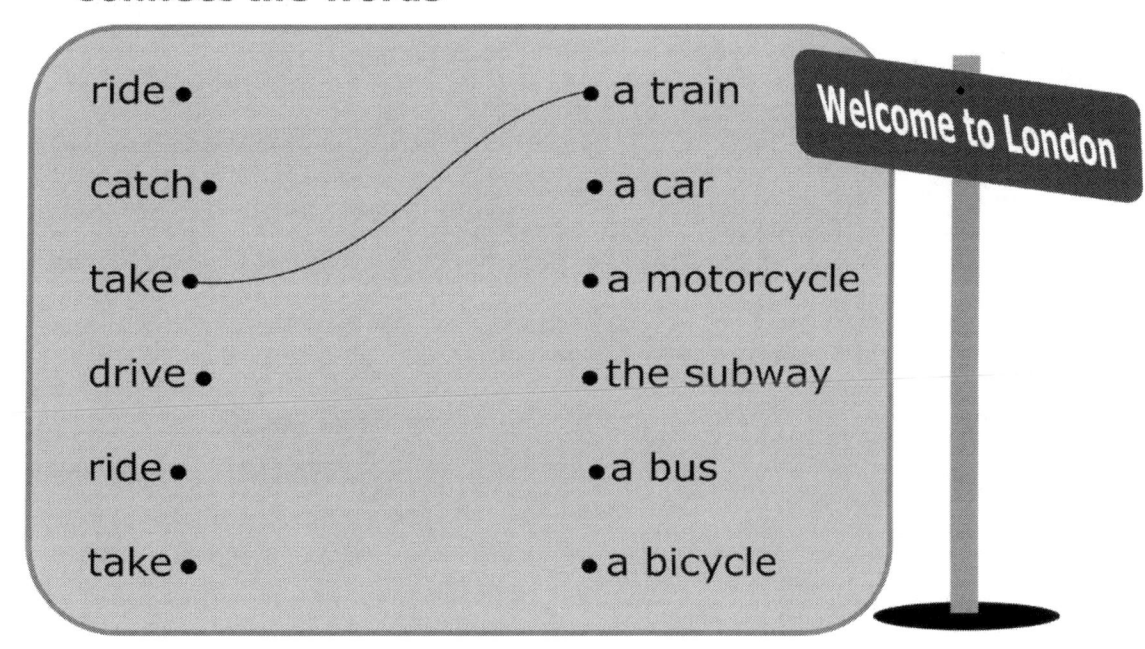

ride •   • a train

catch •   • a car

take •   • a motorcycle

drive •   • the subway

ride •   • a bus

take •   • a bicycle

Lesson 28: Clothes

لباس ها

Section A — Words

1. T-shirt
تی شرت
2. blouse
بلوز
3. scarf
روسری
4. coat
کت
5. dress
لباس
6. hat
کلاه
7. sweater
ژاکت
8. jacket
ژاکت
9. skirt
دامن
10. necktie
کراوات

Section B — Make a sentence

Whose <u>T-shirt</u> is this?

It's <u>mine</u>.

It's not <u>hers</u>.

Whose <u>hat</u> is that?

It's <u>yours</u>.

It's not <u>his</u>.

Learn: mine, yours, his, hers, theirs, ours

Section C | Make a question

Is this your <u>sweater</u>?

Yes, it is. / No, it isn't.

Is this her <u>blouse</u>?

Yes, it is. / No, it isn't.

Alternative: **Yes, it is her blouse.**

Section D | Learn a verb

wear – wearing – wore – worn پوشیدن

You should **wear** a jacket today.

I don't like **wearing** a necktie.

She **wore** a skirt to school yesterday.

My sister hasn't **worn** a dress for a long time.

Section E | Learn an idiom

Wear somebody out

Meaning: To make someone tired.

"My boss completely *wore me out* today."

| Section F | Write |

Trace and fill in the words

1. Whose _____ is _____?

It's _____ mine.

2. _____ blouse _____ that?

_____ hers.

3. Whose _____ _____ this?

_____ his.

4. _____ scarf _____ that?

It's _____ ours.

5. Is _____ your _____?

_____, _____ isn't.

6. _____ this _____ coat?

_____, it _____ my _____.

7. _____ _____ his jacket?

No, _____ _____.

8. _____ that her _____?

Yes, _____ _____ her _____.

Section G | Let's have fun

Clothes!

Write the answer

1. Whose skirt is this? _____.

2. Whose T-shirt is that? _____.

3. Whose necktie is this? _____.

4. Whose jacket is that? _____.

Complete the words

j__ck__t

bl__u__e

__o__t

sk__r__

d__e__s

swe__t__r

n__c__t__e

Is or Are?

1. _____ this your sweater?

Yes, it _____.

2. _____ that her T-shirt?

No, it _____ not.

3. _____ these his shoes?

Yes, they _____.

4. _____ those their jackets?

No, they _____ not.

Test 7   Lesson 25 - 28

Write the answer next to the letter "A"

A: ___ 1. What ___ he cleaning? He was ___ the blender.

a. is, clean   b. can, cleans   c. was, cleaning   d. is, cleaned

A: ___ 2. ___ they cleaning the cupboard? Yes, ___ were.

a. Are, we   b. Can, there   c. Were, they   d. Do, they

A: ___ 3. They ___ the stove yesterday morning.

a. clean   b. cleaned   c. cleans   d. is cleaning

A: ___ 4. "It's difficult because there are too many ___ in the kitchen."

a. cooks   b. cook   c. cooking   d. cooked

A: ___ 5. She was ___ a hammer to fix the fence.

a. use   b. using   c. uses   d. used

A: ___ 6. Was he ___ the axe to fix the tree? No, he ___.

a. using, wasn't   b. use, can't   c. uses, doesn't   d. used, isn't

A: ___ 7. He ___ the pliers every Thursday.

a. use   b. using   c. uses   d. was use

A: ___ 8. "These important things are all my ___ of the trade."

a. work   b. stuff   c. jobs   d. tools

A: ___ **9.** How will he be ___ to New York?

a. go　　　　　b. goes　　　　c. went　　　　d. going

A: ___ **10.** ___ you be ___ a taxi to Sydney? Yes, I will be.

a. Can, take　b. Are, riding　c. Will, taking　d. Do, takes

A: ___ **11.** They ___ a ferry to Hong Kong last night.

a. took　　　　b. taken　　　c. taking　　　d. takes

A: ___ **12.** "I wasn't thinking clearly, I lost my ___ of thought."

a. taxi　　　　b. mind　　　　c. train　　　　d. take

A: ___ **13.** ___ blouse is this? It's ___.

a. Who, my　b. Whose, mine　c. Wear, on　d. Who is, my

A: ___ **14.** Is that ___ jacket? Yes, ___ is.

a. she, it　　b. her, it　　c. him, this　　d. his, they

A: ___ **15.** She was ___ a skirt at school yesterday.

a. wear　　　b. wore　　　c. wears　　　d. wearing

A: ___ **16.** "Doing my homework was tiring. It wore me ___."

a. over　　　b. on　　　　c. in　　　　d. out

Answers on page 206

Lesson 29: More clothes

لباس های بیشتر

Whose jeans are these?
They're mine.

Section A — Words

1. **pants**
   شلوار
2. **shorts**
   شلوار کوتاه
3. **shoes**
   کفش
4. **dresses**
   لباس
5. **shirts**
   پیراهن
6. **jeans**
   شلوار جین
7. **socks**
   جوراب
8. **gloves**
   دستکش
9. **pajamas**
   لباس خواب
10. **boots**
    چکمه

Section B — Make a sentence

Whose <u>pants</u> are these?

They're <u>mine</u>.

They're not <u>his</u>.

Whose <u>jeans</u> are those?

They're <u>hers</u>.

They're not <u>ours</u>.

Note: They're = They are

Section C — Make a question

Are these <u>shoes</u> <u>yours</u>?
Yes, they are. / No, they aren't.

Are those <u>socks</u> <u>his</u>?
Yes, they are. / No, they aren't.

Alternative: **Yes, they are his socks.**

Section D — Learn a verb

lend – lending – lent – lent قرض دادن

I will **lend** my shirt to you.

He is **lending** me his gloves.

My mother **lent** her eraser to me.

I have **lent** my shovel to him before.

Section E — Learn an idiom

Fits like a glove

Meaning: Something is the right size.

"The new shirt you bought me *fits like a glove*."

| Section F | Write |

Trace and fill in the words

1. _____ jeans _____ these?

They're not _____.

2. Whose shorts _____ _____?

_____ hers.

3. _____ socks are _____?

_____ not _____.

4. _____ shoes _____ those?

_____ hers.

5. Are _____ gloves yours?

_____, _____ aren't.

6. _____ _____ dresses hers?

_____, they _____.

7. _____ _____ pajamas _____?

Yes, _____ _____ his _____.

8. _____ those _____ mine?

No, _____ _____.

| Section G | Let's have fun |

More clothes!

Write the answer

1. Whose dresses are those? _____.
2. Whose pants are these? _____.
3. Whose skirts are those? _____.
4. Whose shoes are these? _____.

Connect the words

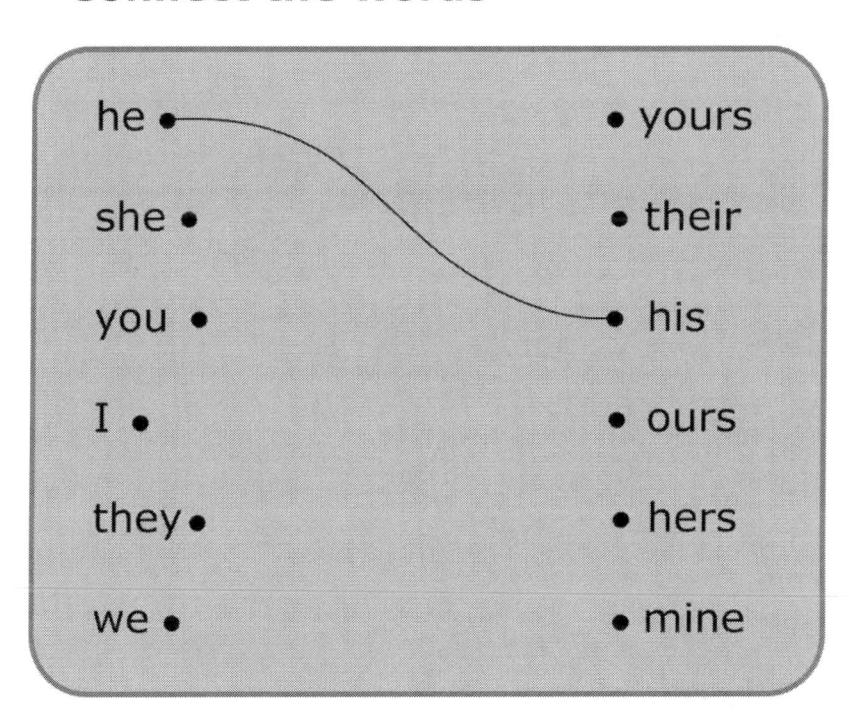

he • — • yours
she • — • their
you • — • his
I • — • ours
they • — • hers
we • — • mine

Complete the words

p___ nts

sh___rt___

s___o___s

sk___rt

dre___s___s

g___ov___s

bo___ts

Lesson 30: In the living room

در اتاق نشیمن

Where is the coffee table?
It's in front of the sofa.

Section A — Words

1. bookcase
   قفسه کتاب
2. television
   تلویزیون
3. clock
   ساعت
4. coffee table
   میز قهوه
5. armchair
   صندلی
6. painting
   تابلو نقاشی
7. TV stand
   میز تلویزیون
8. rug
   فرش
9. sofa
   کاناپه
10. vase
    گلدان

Section B — Make a sentence

Where is the <u>bookcase</u>?

It's <u>next to</u> the <u>sofa</u>.

It's not <u>in front of</u> the <u>armchair</u>.

Where are the <u>book</u>s?

They're <u>under</u> the <u>vase</u>.

They're not <u>behind</u> the <u>television</u>.

Learn: in front of, behind, next to, on, under

Section C — Make a question

Is there a <u>vase</u> on the <u>coffee table</u>?
Yes, there is. / No, there isn't.

Are there <u>pen</u>s behind the <u>TV stand</u>?
Yes, there are. / No, there aren't.

Alternative: **Yes, there are pens there.**

Section D — Learn a verb

move – moving – moved – moved حرکت کردن

After dinner, I will **move** the coffee table.

They are **moving** the armchair next to the sofa.

Dad **moved** the television to the bedroom last night.

We still haven't **moved** the bookcase to the living room.

Section E — Learn an idiom

A race against the clock

Meaning: To not have too much time left to complete a task.

"It's *a race against the clock* to finish this project."

| Section F | Write |

Trace and fill in the words

1. Where _____ _____ television?
   _____ in front _____ the _____.

2. _____ _____ the paintings?
   _____ next _____ the _____.

3. _____ is the _____?
   _____ not behind the _____.

4. _____ _____ the vases?
   _____ not in _____ of the _____.

5. _____ there a cup on _____ bookcase?
   No, _____ _____.

6. Are _____ pencils on _____ coffee _____?
   No, _____ _____.

7. _____ _____ a notebook on the _____?
   Yes, _____ is a _____ there.

8. _____ _____ books _____ the rug?
   Yes, _____ are _____ _____.

Section G | Let's have fun

In the living room!

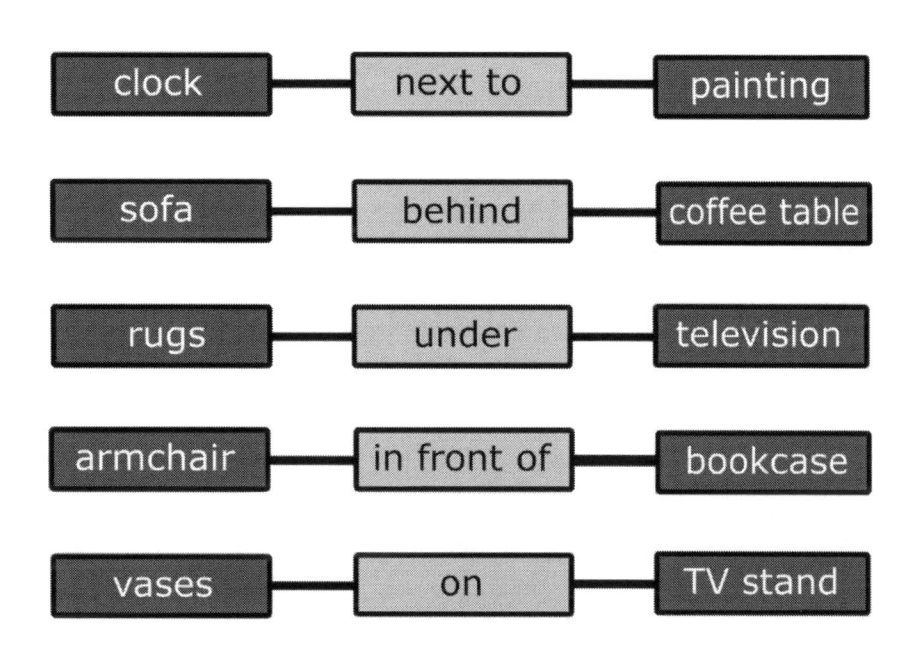

clock	next to	painting
sofa	behind	coffee table
rugs	under	television
armchair	in front of	bookcase
vases	on	TV stand

Answer the questions

1. Where is the clock?
_____.

2. Where is the sofa?
_____.

3. Where are the rugs?
_____.

4. Where is the armchair?
_____.

5. Where are the vases?
_____.

Choose the correct answer

1. Is there a clock next to the painting?
   ☑ Yes, there is.   ○ No, there isn't.

2. Is there a sofa behind the coffee table?
   ○ Yes, there is.   ○ No, there isn't.

3. Are there rugs under the bookcase?
   ○ Yes, there are.   ○ No, there aren't.

4. Is there an armchair in front of the sofa?
   ○ Yes, there is.   ○ No, there isn't.

5. Are there vases on the TV stand?
   ○ Yes, there are.   ○ No, there aren't.

Lesson 31: In the bathroom

در حمام

What is above the sink?
There is a mirror above the sink.

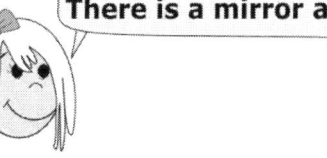

Section A | Words

1. mirror
آینه
2. bath towel
حوله حمام
3. shower
دوش
4. toilet paper
کاغذ توالت
5. bath mat
خشک کن حمام

6. shelf
تاقچه
7. sink
فرو رفتن
8. toilet
توالت فرنگی
9. bathtub
وان حمام
10. soap
صابون

Section B | Make a sentence

What is <u>beside</u> the <u>bathtub</u>?

There is <u>soap</u> beside the bathtub.

There isn't any <u>toilet paper</u> beside the bathtub.

What are <u>on</u> the <u>shelf</u>?

There are some <u>towel</u>s on the shelf.

There aren't any <u>bath mats</u> on the shelf.

Section C | Make a question

Is there a <u>shelf</u> <u>below</u> the <u>mirror</u>?
Yes, there is. / No, there isn't.

Is there <u>toilet paper</u> <u>beside</u> the <u>toilet</u>?
Yes, there is. / No, there isn't.

Alternative: **Yes, there is toilet paper there.**

Section D | Learn a verb

wash – washing – washed – washed شستن

She **washes** the sink every day.

He was **washing** his hands with the new soap.

Kevin **washed** the bath towel this morning.

I won't have **washed** the bath mat by tomorrow.

Section E | Learn an idiom

Throw in the towel

Meaning: To give up or quit.

"After trying three times, he decided to *throw in the towel*."

| Section F | Write |

Trace and fill in the words

1. _____ is _____ the mirror?

   _____ is a _____ below the _____.

2. What _____ beside _____ bath _____?

   There _____ a bathtub _____ the _____ mat.

3. _____ is _____ _____ toilet?

   There _____ a shelf beside the _____.

4. What _____ above _____ shower?

   _____ is a shelf _____ the _____.

5. Is _____ a showerhead _____ the bathtub?

   No, _____ _____.

6. _____ there a _____ above _____ toilet?

   Yes, _____ is a mirror _____.

7. Is _____ a bath towel _____ to the _____?

   _____, _____ isn't.

8. _____ _____ a sink beside the _____?

   _____, _____ is a _____ _____.

| Section G | Let's have fun |

In the bathroom!

There is a mirror above the sink.
There are some bath towels on the shelf.
There aren't any towels in the bathroom.
There is a toilet beside the bathtub.
There isn't any soap in the bathroom.
There is a bath mat under the sink.

Read the information above. Choose the correct answer

1. Is there a mirror above the sink?   ✓ Yes, there is   ○ No, there isn't
2. Are there bath towels on the shelf?   ○ Yes, there are   ○ No, there aren't
3. Are there any towels in the bathroom?   ○ Yes, there are   ○ No, there aren't
4. Is there a toilet beside the bathtub?   ○ Yes, there is   ○ No, there isn't
5. Is there any soap in the bathroom?   ○ Yes, there is   ○ No, there isn't
6. Is there a bath mat under the sink?   ○ Yes, there is   ○ No, there isn't

Complete the words

m__rr __r   t__il __t

b__th__ub   to__l__t p__per

s__ow__r   sh__l__

s__a__   b__t__ to__el

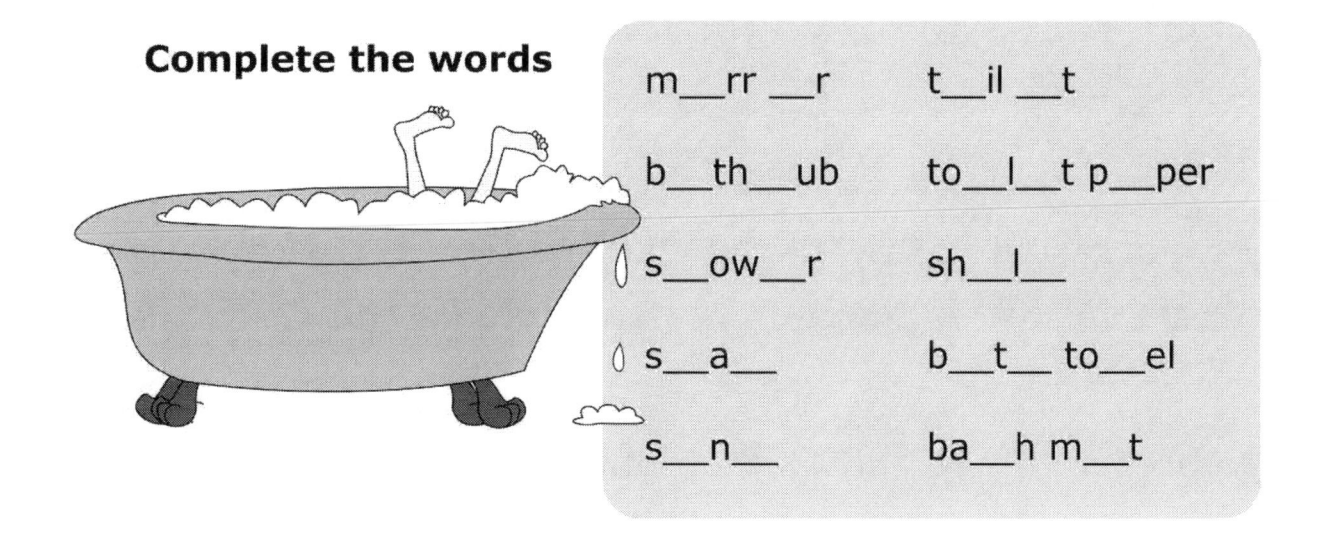

s__n__   ba__h m__t

Lesson 32: In the bedroom

در اتاق خواب

> What is on the left of the bed?
> There is a lamp on the left of the bed.

Section A — Words

1. **bed**
   بستر
2. **pillow**
   بالش
3. **mattress**
   تشک
4. **blanket**
   پتو
5. **drawers**
   دراور
6. **lamp**
   چراغ
7. **alarm clock**
   ساعت زنگدار
8. **wardrobe**
   جارختی
9. **bed sheets**
   تخت
10. **nightstand**
    تختخواب

Section B — Make a sentence

What is <u>on the left of</u> the <u>bed</u>?

There is a <u>lamp</u> on the left of the bed.

There isn't a <u>pillow</u> on the left of the bed.

What are <u>on the right of</u> the <u>wardrobe</u>?

There are <u>drawers</u> on the right of the wardrobe.

There aren't <u>bed sheets</u> on the right of the wardrobe.

Learn: on the left of, on the right of

Section C — Make a question

Is there a <u>nightstand</u> <u>on the left of</u> the <u>bed</u>?
Yes, there is. / No, there isn't.

Are there <u>pillows</u> <u>on the left of</u> the <u>bed</u>?
Yes, there are. / No, there aren't.

Alternative: **Yes, there are pillows on the left of the bed.**

Section D — Learn a verb

change – changing – changed – changed عوض کردن

My brother needs to **change** his bed sheets soon.
We will be **changing** our mattress for a harder one.
I **changed** my pillow last night and slept much better.
I haven't **changed** the light bulb in this lamp for two years.

Section E — Learn an idiom

Get up on the wrong side of the bed

Meaning: To describe somebody who is in a bad mood.

"Mom's in a really bad mood. I think she *got up on the wrong side of the bed*."

| Section F | Write |

Trace and fill in the words

1. _____ is _____ the _____ of the _____?

There _____ a _____ on the right of _____ bed.

2. What _____ on the _____ of _____ nightstand?

_____ is a book _____ the left of the _____.

3. _____ is _____ the right of the _____?

_____ is a _____ on the _____ of the wardrobe.

4. _____ _____ on the _____ of the bed?

There _____ a _____ on the left of the _____.

5. Is _____ a nightstand on the _____ of the bed?

No, _____ isn't.

6. _____ there blankets on the _____ of the _____?

Yes, _____ are _____ on the left of the mattress.

7. _____ there a _____ on the right of the _____?

No, _____ _____.

8. Are there _____ on the left of the _____?

Yes, _____ _____.

Section G — Let's have fun

In the bedroom!

Write the answers

| alarm clock | bed | drawers |

1. What is on the left of the bed?

_____.

2. Are the drawers on the right of the bed?

_____.

| blanket | mattress | pillow |

1. What is on the right of the mattress?

_____.

2. Is the pillow on the left of the mattress?

_____.

| bed sheets | wardrobe | lamp |

1. What is on the left of the wardrobe?

_____.

2. Is the lamp on the left of the wardrobe?

_____.

Test 8 — Lesson 29 - 32

Write the answer next to the letter "A"

A: ___ 1. ___ jeans are those? Those jeans are ___.

a. Whose, hers   b. Who, her   c. Wear, on   d. Whose, her

A: ___ 2. ___ those gloves his? Yes, ___ are.

a. Are, there   b. Are, they   c. Were, them   d. Do, they

A: ___ 3. Can you ___ me your boots?

a. lent   b. lending   c. lend   d. has lent

A: ___ 4. "The new shirt fits perfectly. It fits like a ___."

a. hat   b. sock   c. boot   d. glove

A: ___ 5. Where ___ the books? ___ under the vase.

a. is, They   b. do, It's   c. are, They're   d. put, It's

A: ___ 6. Is ___ a vase on the coffee table? No, there ___.

a. it, wasn't   b. there, isn't   c. there, doesn't   d. he, isn't

A: ___ 7. He hasn't ___ that new television yet.

a. move   b. moving   c. moves   d. moved

A: ___ 8. "We don't have much time. We have to race against the ___."

a. clock   b. watch   c. car   d. team

A: ___ **9.** There ___ a bath mat ___ the bathtub.

a. are, above   b. have, on   c. be, in   d. is, beside

A: ___ **10.** Are ___ towels beside the mirror? No, there ___.

a. them, can't   b. there, aren't   c. have, hasn't   d. it, isn't

A: ___ **11.** He ___ the sink every Saturday afternoon.

a. wash   b. washing   c. washes   d. is wash

A: ___ **12.** "After failing many times, I decided to throw in the ___."

a. towel   b. quit   c. anger   d. ball

A: ___ **13.** There ___ drawers on the ___ of the wardrobe.

a. have, top   b. is, side   c. can, right   d. are, left

A: ___ **14.** Is ___ a lamp on the left of the bed? Yes, there ___.

a. it, have   b. there, is   c. they're, are   d. his, can

A: ___ **15.** We will ___ the blankets tomorrow.

a. changes   b. changing   c. change   d. changed

A: ___ **16.** "He's grumpy. I think he got up on the wrong side of the ___.

a. bed   b. lamp   c. happy   d. clock

Answers on page 206

Lesson 33: Around the house

در اطراف خانه

What will he be doing this weekend?
He will be fixing the gate.

Section A — Words

1. **work in the garage**
   کار کردن در گاراژ
2. **fix the mailbox**
   صندوق پستی را تعمیر کنید
3. **fix the gate**
   دروازه را تعمیر کن
4. **work in the garden**
   کار در باغ
5. **clean the pool**
   تمیز کردن استخر
6. **work in the yard**
   کار کردن در حیاط
7. **fix the fence**
   نرده را تعمیر کنید
8. **clean the balcony**
   بالکن را تمیز کنید
9. **clean the outdoor furniture**
   تمیز کردن مبلمان فضای باز
10. **clean the barbecue**
    کباب را تمیز کنید

Section B — Make a sentence

What will he be doing <u>this weekend</u>?

He'll be <u>working in the garage</u>.

He won't be <u>cleaning the barbecue</u>.

What won't she be doing <u>this weekend</u>?

She won't be <u>fixing the mailbox</u>.

She'll be <u>cleaning the outdoor furniture</u>.

Note: won't be = will not be, he'll = he will, she'll = she will

Section C — Make a question

Will he be <u>working in the garden</u> <u>tomorrow</u>?
Yes, he will be. / No, he won't be.

Will you be <u>fixing the gate</u> <u>tomorrow</u>?
Yes, I will be. / No, I won't be.

Alternative: **Yes, I'll be fixing it.**

Section D — Learn a verb

fix – fixing – fixed – fixed تعمیر کردن

He **fixes** the fence every year.

My father is **fixing** the gate right now.

My uncle **fixed** our mailbox after the big storm last week.

I still haven't **fixed** the grammar mistakes in my report.

Section E — Learn an idiom

On the house

Meaning: To get something for free.

"The waiter apologized and gave him the meal *on the house*."

Section F — Write

Trace and fill in the words

1. _____ will _____ be _____ this _____?

   She'll be _____ in _____ yard.

2. What will _____ be _____ _____ weekend?

   _____ be _____ _____ fence.

3. What _____ they be _____ this _____?

   _____ _____ cleaning the _____.

4. _____ will _____ be doing _____ _____?

   He _____ fixing _____ gate.

5. Will _____ be _____ in the garden _____?

   _____, he won't _____.

6. Will we _____ _____ the pool tomorrow?

   _____, _____ will _____.

7. _____ you be working in the _____ _____?

   Yes, _____ _____ _____.

8. Will they _____ cleaning the barbecue _____?

   No, _____ _____ _____.

Section G | Let's have fun

Around the house!

doing	weekend	this	
be	will	the	working

Write the words

What _____ she be doing this weekend?

She will _____ cleaning the balcony.

What will they be _____ this _____?

They will be fixing _____ fence.

What will you be doing _____ weekend?

I will be _____ in the yard.

don't, doesn't, didn't, won't, isn't, aren't, wasn't, weren't?

do not = __don't__   were not = _____

did not = _____   are not = _____

will not = _____   does not = _____

is not = _____   was not = _____

Lesson 34: Hobbies

سرگرمی

> What do you enjoy doing on the weekend?
> I enjoy going hiking.

Section A — Words

1. **do gardening**
   باغبانی کردن
2. **go hiking**
   پیاده روی
3. **take photographs**
   عکس گرفتن
4. **play video games**
   بازی های ویدئویی بازی کنید
5. **listen to music**
   گوش دادن به موسیقی
6. **go camping**
   به کمپینگ رفتن
7. **play chess**
   شطرنج بازی کردن
8. **watch movies**
   تماشای فیلم ها
9. **go fishing**
   ماهیگیری
10. **sing karaoke**
    خواندن کارائوکه

Section B — Make a sentence

What do you enjoy doing on the weekend?

I enjoy <u>doing gardening</u> on the weekend.

I don't enjoy <u>playing video games</u> on the weekend.

What does he enjoy doing on the weekend?

He enjoys <u>going camping</u> on the weekend.

He doesn't enjoy <u>singing karaoke</u> on the weekend.

| Section C | Make a question |

Do you enjoy <u>going hiking</u> on the weekend?
Yes, I do. / No, I enjoy <u>playing chess</u>.

Does he enjoy <u>watching movies</u> on the weekend?
Yes, he does. / No, he enjoys <u>going fishing</u>.

Alternative: **Yes, he does enjoy watching movies.**

| Section D | Learn a verb |

enjoy – enjoying – enjoyed – enjoyed لذت بردن

He **enjoys** doing the gardening in spring.

My aunt is **enjoying** the book you lent her.

I really **enjoyed** the movie we watched last night.

You would have **enjoyed** the video game we played today.

| Section E | Learn an idiom |

Face the music

Meaning: To face the consequences of one's actions.

"You need to own up to your mistake and *face the music*."

Section F   Write

Trace and fill in the words

1. What _____ you _____ doing on the _____?

   _____ enjoy _____ camping on _____ weekend.

2. _____ does _____ enjoy doing on the _____?

   She _____ _____ hiking _____ the weekend.

3. _____ do they enjoy _____ on the _____?

   _____ enjoy _____ karaoke on the _____.

4. What _____ he enjoy _____ on the _____?

   _____ _____ _____ chess on the _____.

5. Do _____ enjoy _____ video games on the weekend?

   No, I _____ listening to _____.

6. _____ he enjoy _____ photographs on the _____?

   _____, _____ does.

7. _____ they _____ going hiking on the _____?

   No, _____ enjoy _____ _____.

8. _____ she enjoy _____ chess on the _____?

   Yes, _____ _____.

Section G | Let's have fun

Hobbies!

Connect the words

listen • • hiking

take • • movies

go • • chess

play • • karaoke

watch • • photographs

sing • • to music

Enjoy or Enjoys?

1. He _____ listening to music on the weekend.

2. They _____ watching movies on the weekend.

3. We _____ going hiking on the weekend.

4. My brother _____ playing chess on the weekend.

5. She _____ taking photographs on the weekend.

6. I _____ playing video games on the weekend.

Answer the questions

1. What do you enjoy doing on the weekend?
   _____.

2. What does your friend enjoy doing on the weekend?
   _____.

Lesson 35: Countries

کشورها

Which countries have you been to?
I have been to Brazil and Mexico.

Section A — Words

1. **Japan**
   ژاپن
2. **Canada**
   کانادا
3. **Brazil**
   برزیل
4. **Australia**
   استرالیا
5. **South Africa**
   آفریقای جنوبی
6. **China**
   چین
7. **Mexico**
   مکزیک
8. **Argentina**
   آرژانتین
9. **New Zealand**
   نیوزلند
10. **Kenya**
    کنیا

Section B — Make a sentence

Which countries have you been to?

I have been to <u>Japan</u> and <u>China</u>.

I haven't been to <u>Australia</u>.

Which countries has she been to?

She has been to <u>Canada</u> and <u>Mexico</u>.

She hasn't been to <u>Kenya</u>.

Note: haven't = have not / hasn't = has not

Section C — Make a question

Have you been to <u>Brazil</u>?
Yes, I have. / No, I haven't.

Has he been to <u>Argentina</u>?
Yes, he has. / No, he hasn't.

Alternative: **Yes, he has been there.**

Section D — Learn a verb

write – writing – wrote – written نوشتن

I always **write** homework on the weekend.
She is **writing** a new book about South Africa.
My father **wrote** a letter to his friend in Japan last week.
He has already **written** four emails to the factory in China.

Section E — Learn an idiom

Second to none

Meaning: To describe something that is the best.

"The mountains in Canada are *second to none* for skiing."

| Section F | Write |

Trace and fill in the words

1. _____ countries _____ you _____ to?
   _____ have _____ to _____ and _____.

2. Which _____ has _____ been _____?
   He _____ been _____ Brazil and _____.

3. _____ countries _____ we _____ _____?
   We _____ been to _____ and _____.

4. Which _____ has she _____ _____?
   _____ _____ been to _____ and _____.

5. _____ you been _____ New Zealand?
   Yes, I _____ been _____.

6. Has _____ been _____ Australia?
   _____, _____ hasn't.

7. _____ they _____ to China?
   Yes, _____ _____ been _____.

8. _____ he _____ _____ Kenya?
   No, _____ _____.

Section G — Let's have fun

Countries!

Write the missing words

| hasn't | they | has | been |
| to | countries | Which | haven't |

1. Which _____ have you been to?

I have _____ to Japan and China.

2. _____ countries has he been to?

He _____ been to Mexico and Canada.

3. Has she been _____ South Africa?

No, she _____.

4. Have _____ been to New Zealand?

No, they _____.

Has or Have?

1. _____ she been to Canada?

Yes, she _____.

2. _____ they been to Mexico?

No, they _____ not.

3. Which countries _____ you been to?

I _____ been to Argentina and Brazil.

4. Which countries _____ he been to?

He _____ been to Kenya and China.

Lesson 36: Landscapes

مناظر طبیعی

> What had you prepared for yesterday's math class?
> I had prepared a video about lakes.

Section A | Words

1. river
رودخانه
2. beach (es)
ساحل دریا
3. mountain
کوه
4. volcano (es)
آتشفشان
5. forest
جنگل
6. lake
دریاچه
7. waterfall
آبشار
8. island
جزیره
9. ocean
اقیانوس
10. jungle
جنگل

Section B | Make a sentence

What had you prepared for yesterday's <u>geography</u> class?

I had prepared a <u>poster</u> about <u>river</u>s.

I hadn't prepared anything about <u>jungle</u>s.

What had they prepared for yesterday's <u>Chinese</u> class?

They had prepared an <u>article</u> about <u>lake</u>s.

They hadn't prepared anything about <u>island</u>s.

Learn: poster, speech, video, article, presentation

Note: hadn't = had not

Section C — Make a question

Had you prepared anything for yesterday's <u>English</u> class?
Yes, I had prepared a <u>speech</u>. / No, I hadn't.

Had you prepared anything for yesterday's <u>science</u> class?
Yes, I had prepared a <u>video</u>. / No, I hadn't.

Alternative: **No, I hadn't prepared anything yet.**

Section D — Learn a verb

prepare – preparing – prepared – prepared آماده شدن

I'll **prepare** some food for you to take to the mountains.

She'll be **preparing** some drinks for the picnic at the lake.

The teacher always **prepared** a quiz for the students before.

I wish I had **prepared** more for the geography test.

Section E — Learn an idiom

A drop in the ocean

Meaning: To only make a tiny impact.

"We donated money to the victims of the tsunami, but I'm afraid it is just *a drop in the ocean*."

| Section F | Write |

Trace and fill in the words

1. What had you _____ for _____ geography _____?

   I _____ prepared an _____ about _____.

2. _____ had he _____ for yesterday's _____ class?

   He _____ prepared a _____ _____ waterfalls.

3. What had they _____ for _____ _____ class?

   They _____ _____ a video _____ mountains.

4. What had you _____ for _____ geography _____?

   _____ _____ _____ a poster _____ islands.

5. Had he _____ _____ for yesterday's _____ class?

   No, _____ _____.

6. _____ you prepared _____ for _____ art class?

   _____, I _____ _____ a poster.

7. Had she _____ anything for _____ _____ class?

   No, _____ _____.

8. _____ he prepared anything for _____ English class?

   Yes, _____ had _____ a _____.

Section G | Let's have fun

Landscapes!

Unscramble the words and write

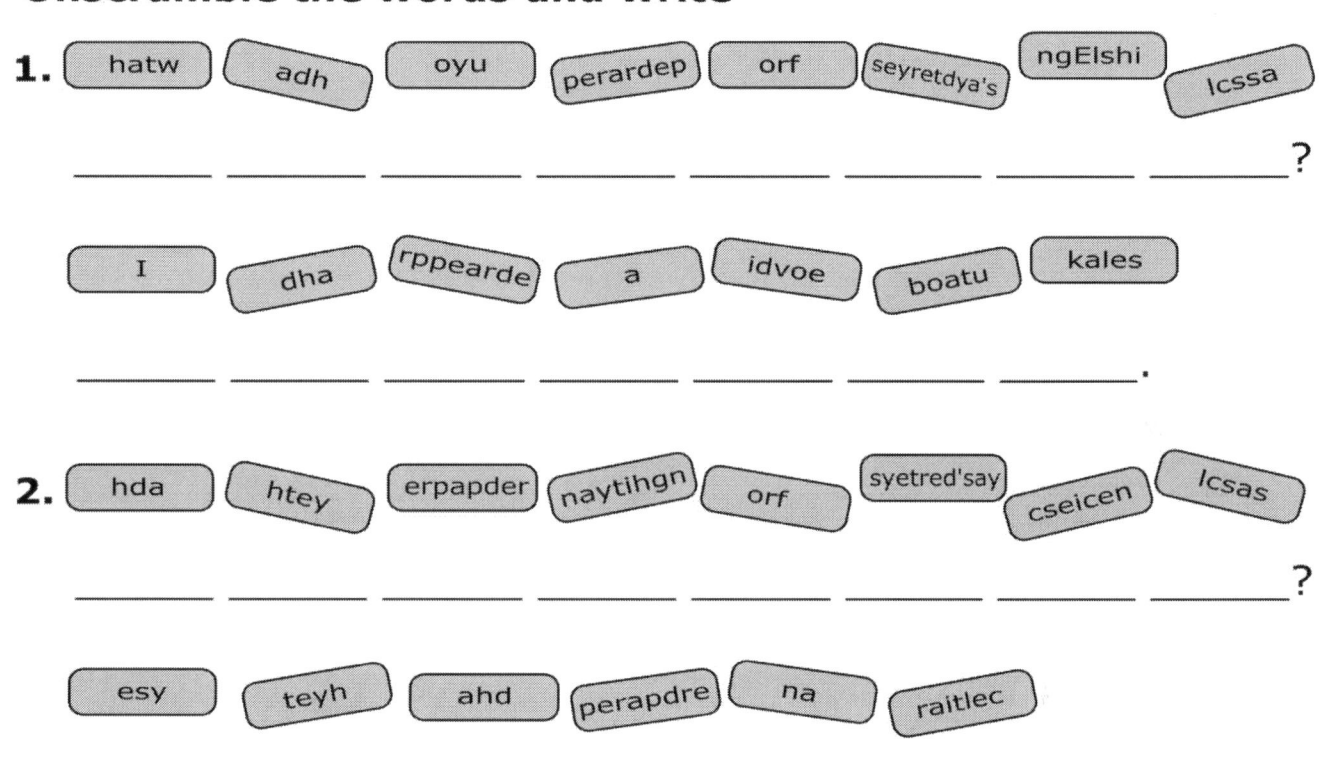

1. hatw | adh | oyu | perardep | orf | seyretdya's | ngElshi | lcssa

   ____ ____ ____ ____ ____ ____ ____ ____ ?

   I | dha | rppearde | a | idvoe | boatu | kales

   ____ ____ ____ ____ ____ ____ ____ .

2. hda | htey | erpapder | naytihgn | orf | syetred'say | cseicen | lcsas

   ____ ____ ____ ____ ____ ____ ____ ____ ?

   esy | teyh | ahd | perapdre | na | raitlec

   ____ , ____ ____ ____ ____ ____ .

Complete the words

r__v__r   j__ng__e

v__l__a__o   i__la__d

m__un__a__n   f__r__ __t

be__c__   w__te__f__l__

o__e__n   l__k__

Test 9 — Lesson 33 - 36

Write the answer next to the letter "A"

A: ___ 1. ___ weekend, he will be ___ the mailbox.

a. On, clean   b. This, fixing   c. That, work   d. In, cleaning

A: ___ 2. ___ she be fixing the gate tonight? Yes, she ___.

a. Can, is   b. Won't, fix   c. Will, will be   d. Will, fix

A: ___ 3. My mother ___ the barbecue last year.

a. fix   b. is fixing   c. fixed   d. will fixing

A: ___ 4. "This one's free. It's on the ___."

a. house   b. yard   c. gate   d. garage

A: ___ 5. He ___ fishing on the weekend.

a. enjoy going   b. is enjoy go   c. enjoys go   d. enjoys going

A: ___ 6. ___ he enjoy watching movies? No, he ___ playing chess.

a. Do, does   b. Is, isn't   c. Does, doesn't   d. Does, enjoys

A: ___ 7. She is ___ her new barbecue.

a. enjoying   b. enjoy   c. enjoys   d. enjoyed

A: ___ 8. "You should admit your mistake and face the ___."

a. sunshine   b. music   c. trouble   d. smile

A: ___ **9.** Which countries ___ you ___ to?

a. have, go   b. did, went   c. do, be   d. have, been

A: ___ **10.** ___ she been to Japan? No, she ___.

a. Has, hasn't   b. Have, don't   c. Is, hasn't   d. Is, can't

A: ___ **11.** He has ___ nine messages this week.

a. write   b. wrote   c. written   d. writes

A: ___ **12.** "Her English is the best. It's second to ___."

a. all   b. none   c. best   d. win

A: ___ **13.** They had ___ a speech for last week's geography class.

a. prepare   b. prepared   c. preparing   d. prepares

A: ___ **14.** ___ he prepared anything for English class? No, he ___.

a. Had, hadn't   b. Is, isn't   c. Does, don't   d. Has, haven't

A: ___ **15.** The teacher always ___ easy tests for his students.

a. prepare   b. preparing   c. prepares   d. are preparing

A: ___ **16.** "It had a very small effect. It was just a drop in the ___."

a. line   b. ball   c. water   d. ocean

Answers on page 206

Lesson 37: Everyday life

زندگی روزمره

> When will you have woken up by?
> I will have woken up by six o'clock.

Section A — Words

1. **woken up**
   بیدار شده ام
2. **brushed my teeth**
   دندان هایم را مسواک زده ام
3. **done homework**
   انجام تکالیف انجام شده
4. **cooked dinner**
   شام پخته شده
5. **taken out the trash**
   حذف سطل زباله
6. **eaten breakfast**
   صبحانه خورده ام
7. **gone to school**
   رفته به مدرسه
8. **taken a shower**
   دوش گرفته شده
9. **gone to sleep**
   رفته به خواب
10. **gone shopping**
    رفته خرید

Section B — Make a sentence

When will you have <u>woken up</u> by?

I will have woken up by <u>seven o'clock</u>.

I won't have woken up by <u>half past six</u>.

When will he have <u>eaten breakfast</u> by?

He will have eaten breakfast by <u>half past eight</u>.

He won't have eaten breakfast by <u>eight o'clock</u>.

Learn: o'clock, half past, a quarter past, a quarter to

170

Section C — Make a question

Will you have <u>taken a shower</u> by <u>nine o'clock</u>?

Yes, I will have. / No, I won't have.

Will they have <u>done homework</u> by <u>a quarter to six</u>?

Yes, they will have. / No, they won't have.

Alternative: **Yes, they will have done homework by then.**

Section D — Learn a verb

wake – waking – woke – woken بیدار شدن

I **wake** up at seven o'clock every day.

The baby is **waking** up now.

You **woke** up late this morning.

I haven't **woken** up this early for years.

Section E — Learn an idiom

Hit the nail on the head

Meaning: To say something that is correct.

"I agree with what you said. You really *hit the nail on the head*."

| Section F | Write |

Trace and fill in the words

1. _____ will you _____ woken _____ by?

I _____ have _____ up by a _____ past seven.

2. When _____ he have _____ his teeth _____?

He _____ have brushed his _____ by half past nine.

3. When _____ you _____ gone to school _____?

I will _____ gone to _____ by ten _____.

4. When will _____ have _____ homework _____?

She will _____ done _____ by _____ o'clock.

5. _____ they _____ cooked _____ by six o'clock?

No, _____ won't _____.

6. Will _____ have gone to sleep by _____ past ten?

Yes, we _____ _____.

7. _____ she _____ gone shopping by nine _____?

No, _____ _____ have.

8. _____ you have brushed _____ teeth by one _____?

Yes, _____ _____ _____.

Section G Let's have fun

Everyday life!

Unscramble the sentences

(o'clock / gone / have / we / will / shopping / by / four)

1. _____.

(two / taken / have / they / will / a shower / by / half past)

2. _____.

(I / the trash / won't / one o'clock / have / by / taken out)

3. _____.

(o'clock / cooked dinner / have / he / won't / by / six)

4. _____.

Connect the words

brushed •   • out the trash

gone •   • dinner

taken •   • my teeth

done •   • a shower

cooked •   • homework

taken •   • to sleep

Lesson 38: Languages

زبان ها

How long have you been learning German?
I have been learning German for one year.

Section A — Words

1. **English**
   انگلیسی
2. **German**
   آلمانی
3. **Portuguese**
   پرتغالی
4. **Japanese**
   ژاپنی
5. **Vietnamese**
   ویتنامی
6. **Spanish**
   اسپانیایی
7. **French**
   فرانسوی
8. **Chinese**
   چینی ها
9. **Hindi**
   هندی
10. **Arabic**
    عربی

Section B — Make a sentence

How long have you been <u>learning</u> <u>English</u>?

I have been learning English for <u>three years</u>.

I haven't been learning English for <u>four years</u>.

How long has he been <u>studying</u> <u>Spanish</u>?

He has been studying Spanish for <u>five months</u>.

He hasn't been studying Spanish for <u>five years</u>.

Learn: learning, studying, speaking

| Section C | Make a question |

Have they been <u>studying</u> <u>French</u> for a long time?
Yes, they have been. / No, they haven't been.

Has she been <u>learning</u> <u>Hindi</u> for a long time?
Yes, she has been. / No, she hasn't been.

Alternative: **Yes, she's been learning Hindi for <u>six years</u>.**

| Section D | Learn a verb |

speak – speaking – spoke – spoken سخن گفتن , صحبت کردن

He **speaks** three languages.

She is **speaking** to him in Japanese.

I **spoke** with my teacher about the German homework.

We haven't **spoken** to each other for over five years.

| Section E | Learn an idiom |

Speak the same language

Meaning: To share the same understanding and be in agreement.

"I agree with everything you are saying. I think we're *speaking the same language*."

| Section F | Write |

Trace and fill in the words

1. How _____ have _____ been _____ _____?

I _____ been learning German _____ three _____.

2. How _____ has _____ been _____ French?

She has _____ studying _____ for _____ years.

3. How _____ have we _____ learning _____?

_____ have been _____ English for three _____.

4. _____ long have _____ been _____ Hindi?

They _____ been learning _____ for _____ year.

5. _____ they been _____ Arabic for a _____ time?

Yes, _____ have _____.

6. _____ he been _____ _____ for a long time?

No, _____ hasn't _____.

7. Have _____ been _____ Arabic for a _____ time?

Yes, I _____ _____.

8. Has she _____ studying _____ for a long _____?

No, _____ _____ _____.

Section G | Let's have fun

Languages!

Mexico France Scotland Japan Egypt

Write the Country, Question and Answer

He — English — Three years — Scotland

How long has he been learning English?
He has been learning English for three years.

They — Spanish — Ten years — _____
_____?
_____.

She — Arabic — Four years — _____
_____?
_____.

John — Japanese — One year — _____
_____?
_____.

Susan — French — Two years — _____
_____?
_____.

How long have you been studying English?
_____.

Lesson 39: Pets

حیوانات خانگی

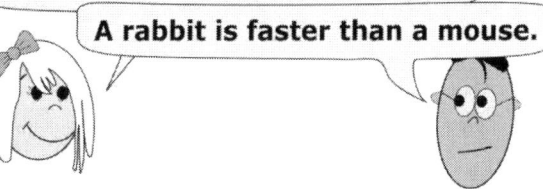

What is faster than a mouse?
A rabbit is faster than a mouse.

Section A — Words

1. **dog**
سگ
2. **fish**
ماهی
3. **bird**
پرنده
4. **rabbit**
خرگوش
5. **guinea pig**
خوک گینه

6. **cat**
گربه
7. **turtle**
لاک پشت
8. **mouse**
موش
9. **hamster**
همستر
10. **snake**
مار

Section B — Make a sentence

What is <u>bigger</u> than a <u>cat</u>?

A <u>dog</u> is bigger than a cat.

A <u>fish</u> isn't bigger than a cat.

What is <u>more expensive</u> than the <u>hamster</u>?

The <u>rabbit</u> is more expensive than the hamster.

The <u>mouse</u> isn't more expensive than the hamster.

Learn: faster, slower, bigger, smaller, more expensive, cheaper, more colorful, better, worse

Section C — Make a question

Is a <u>turtle</u> <u>slower</u> than a <u>guinea pig</u>?

Yes, it is. / No, it's not. It's <u>faster</u>.

Is the <u>bird</u> <u>more expensive</u> than the <u>snake</u>?

Yes, it is. / No, it's not. It's <u>cheaper</u>.

Alternative: **Yes, it is more expensive.**

Section D — Learn a verb

feed – feeding – fed – fed   خوراک دادن

You need to **feed** the dog every morning.

He is **feeding** the turtle some leaves.

I **fed** the mouse some cheese and it happily ate it.

My sister hasn't **fed** the pets today.

Section E — Learn an idiom

The teacher's pet

Meaning: A student whom the teacher favors.

"Her classmates are jealous of her because she is *the teacher's pet*."

Section F — Write

Trace and fill in the words

1. _____ is bigger _____ a _____?

   A _____ is _____ than _____ mouse.

2. What _____ more _____ _____ the dog?

   The fish is _____ colorful _____ the _____.

3. _____ _____ slower _____ a _____?

   A turtle is _____ _____ a cat.

4. _____ is less _____ _____ the snake?

   _____ bird is _____ expensive than the _____.

5. _____ the bird faster _____ the guinea pig?

   Yes, _____ _____.

6. Is _____ rabbit more _____ than the _____?

   No, _____ _____. It's cheaper.

7. _____ the turtle slower than the _____?

   _____, _____ is _____.

8. Is the _____ slower _____ the hamster?

   _____, it's _____. It's _____.

Section G — Let's have fun

Pets!

Write the animals

Animal	Speed	Size
_____	48 km/h	30 cm
_____	0.4 km/h	40 cm
_____	13 km/h	9 cm
_____	5 km/h	15 cm

Answer the questions

1. What is bigger than a fish? _____.

2. What is faster than a mouse? _____.

3. Is the turtle faster than the fish? _____.

4. Is the mouse slower than the rabbit? _____.

5. What is bigger than a rabbit? _____.

6. What is smaller than a fish? _____.

7. Is the rabbit bigger than the turtle? _____.

8. Is the rabbit bigger than the fish? _____.

Lesson 40: Fast food

فست فود

What is the sweetest food?
The sweetest food is the pancake.

Section A — Words

1. doughnut
دونات
2. cheeseburger
چیزبرگر
3. chicken nuggets
ناگت مرغ
4. pancake
پنکیک
5. taco
تاکو
6. french fries
سیب زمینی سرخ کرده
7. onion rings
حلقه های پیاز
8. hot dog
هات داگ
9. fried chicken
مرغ سرخ شده
10. burrito
بوریتو

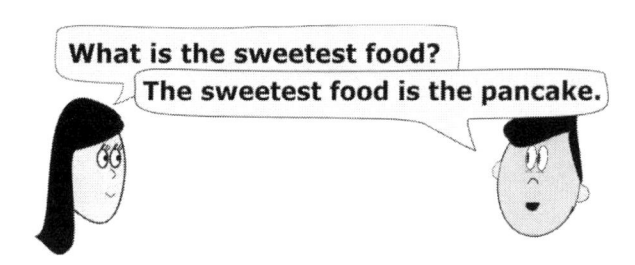

Section B — Make a sentence

What is the <u>cheapest</u> food?

The cheapest food is the <u>doughnut</u>.

The cheapest food isn't the <u>cheeseburger</u>.

What is the <u>most expensive</u> food?

The most expensive food is the <u>burrito</u>.

The most expensive food isn't the <u>fried chicken</u>.

Learn: most delicious, most expensive, cheapest, saltiest, sweetest, best, worst

| Section C | Make a question |

Is the <u>hot dog</u> the <u>most delicious</u>?
Yes, it is. / No, it's not.

Are the <u>french fries</u> the <u>cheapest</u>?
Yes, they are. / No, they aren't.

Alternative: **Yes, they are the cheapest.**

| Section D | Learn a verb |

try – trying – tried – tried سعی کردن

He wants to **try** the cheeseburger at that restaurant.

I'm **trying** to decide whether to buy the taco or burrito.

My baby brother **tried** the pancake, but didn't like it.

We haven't **tried** the fried chicken here yet.

| Section E | Learn an idiom |

You are what you eat

Meaning: The food that you eat affects your health.

"Careful not to eat too much fast food. *You are what you eat.*"

| Section F | Write |

Trace and fill in the words

1. _____ is _____ cheapest _____?

The _____ food _____ the _____.

2. What _____ the _____ _____?

_____ best _____ is _____ burrito.

3. _____ is the _____ delicious food?

_____ most _____ food _____ the _____.

4. _____ _____ the _____ food?

_____ worst _____ is _____ hot dog.

5. _____ _____ cheeseburger the _____ expensive?

No, _____ _____.

6. _____ the french _____ the _____?

Yes, _____ _____ _____ saltiest.

7. Is the _____ chicken _____ _____ delicious?

Yes, _____ _____ the most _____.

8. Is _____ pancake _____ worst?

_____, it's _____.

Section G — Let's have fun

Fast food!

Joe's Diner

doughnut	$2	french fries	$5
cheeseburger	$4	onion rings	$6
chicken nugget	$1	hot dog	$3
pancake	$6	fried chicken	$7
taco	$8	burrito	$9

Answer the questions

1. What is the most expensive food? _____.

2. What is the cheapest food? _____.

3. What is the saltiest food? _____.

4. What is the sweetest food? _____.

5. What is the most delicious food? _____.

6. Is the pancake the sweetest food? _____.

7. Is the taco the most delicious food? _____.

8. Are the french fries the saltiest food? _____.

Test 10   Lesson 37 - 40

Write the answer next to the letter "A"

A: ___ 1. When ___ you have ___ to school by?

a. do, go   b. will, gone   c. can, went   d. will, go

A: ___ 2. They will have ___ dinner by ___ six.

a. eat, o'clock   b. ate, past   c. eats, quarter   d. eaten, half past

A: ___ 3. They haven't ___ with each other for two years.

a. spoken   b. spokes   c. speaking   d. speaks

A: ___ 4. "You said it exactly right. You hit the ___ on the head."

a. hammer   b. work   c. nail   d. day

A: ___ 5. How long ___ he ___ learning Arabic?

a. does, is   b. is, can   c. have, does   d. has, been

A: ___ 6. No, ___ haven't been ___ Spanish for a long time.

a. I, learn   b. we, learned   c. they, learning   d. he, learns

A: ___ 7. He ___ Chinese with the doctor last night.

a. spoke   b. is   c. was   d. speaks

A: ___ 8. "I really agree with him. I think we ___ the same language."

a. speaks   b. speak   c. spoken   d. speaking

A: ___ **9.** What is ___ than a guinea pig?

a. cheaper	b. more cheap	c. more cheaper	d. cheapest

A: ___ **10.** Is the mouse ___ than the cat? No, it's ___.

a. slow, slower	b. big, smaller	c. slow, fast	d. slower, faster

A: ___ **11.** We haven't ___ the pets yet.

a. feed	b. fed	c. feeding	d. feeds

A: ___ **12.** "The teacher really loved him. He was the teacher's ___."

a. pets	b. petting	c. pet	d. best

A: ___ **13.** What is the ___ food on the menu?

a. more cheap	b. cheapest	c. most cheap	d. cheapen

A: ___ **14.** ___ the taco the ___ delicious?

a. Had, more	b. Is, more	c. Does, most	d. Is, most

A: ___ **15.** He usually ___ new food every weekend.

a. try	b. trying	c. tries	d. had try

A: ___ **16.** "You should eat healthier food. You ___ what you eat."

a. are	b. can	c. do	d. try

Answers on page 206

Lesson 41: At the cinema

در سینما

> What was the romance movie like?
>
> It was romantic.

Section A — Words

1. **scary**
   ترسناک
2. **exciting**
   هیجان انگیز
3. **informative**
   آموزنده
4. **romantic**
   رومانتیک
5. **violent**
   خشن
6. **boring**
   بر سر حوصله
7. **interesting**
   جالب
8. **funny**
   خنده دار
9. **enjoyable**
   لذت بخش
10. **sad**
    غمگین

Section B — Make a sentence

What was the <u>horror</u> movie like?

It was <u>scary</u>.

It wasn't <u>enjoyable</u>.

What was the <u>action</u> movie like?

It was <u>exciting</u>.

It wasn't <u>boring</u>.

Learn: horror, comedy, action, romance, sci-fi, animation

Section C — Make a question

Was the <u>horror</u> movie as <u>exciting</u> as the <u>action</u> movie?
Yes, it was. / No, it wasn't.

Was the <u>sci-fi</u> movie as <u>funny</u> as the <u>comedy</u> movie?
Yes, it was. / No, it wasn't.

Alternative: **Yes, it was as funny as the comedy movie.**

Section D — Learn a verb

teach – teaching – taught – taught تدریس کردن

The movie **teaches** us about looking after the environment.

My father will be **teaching** me how to swim.

My history teacher **taught** us interesting things this year.

The teacher hasn't **taught** us anything informative yet.

Section E — Learn an idiom

A tough act to follow

Meaning: Someone who did so well that it would be hard to do better.

"He was so funny in this movie. It will be *a tough act to follow*."

Section F — Write

Trace and fill in the words

1. _____ was _____ comedy _____ like?

   It _____ _____.

2. What _____ the romance movie _____?

   _____ was _____.

3. _____ _____ the _____ movie like?

   _____ _____ exciting.

4. What _____ _____ animation movie _____?

   It _____ _____.

5. Was the _____ movie as funny as the _____ movie?

   No, _____ _____.

6. Was the action movie as _____ as the _____ movie?

   Yes, _____ _____.

7. _____ the _____ movie as sad as the sci-fi movie?

   _____, _____ wasn't.

8. Was the _____ _____ as violent as the action movie?

   _____, it _____.

Section G | Let's have fun

At the cinema!

> What was the comedy movie like?
> It was funny.

> What was the action movie like?
> It was exciting.

> What was the sci-fi movie like?
> It was interesting.

> What was the romance movie like?
> It was boring.

True of False? Circle the answer

1. The comedy movie was funny.   True   False
2. The romance movie was informative.   True   False
3. The action movie was exciting.   True   False
4. The sci-fi movie was sad.   True   False

Complete the words

b__r__ng	i__fo__ma__i__e	e__jo__ab__e
i__t__r__s__in__	e__c__tin__	sc__r__
f__n__y	r__m__nt__c	v__o__en__

Lesson 42: Music

موسیقی

> How does she play the violin?
> She plays the violin gracefully.

Section A — Words

1. **beautifully**
   زیبایی
2. **quietly**
   بی سر و صدا
3. **slowly**
   به آرامی
4. **gracefully**
   با شکوه
5. **well**
   خوب
6. **loudly**
   با صدای بلند
7. **quickly**
   به سرعت
8. **terribly**
   وحشتناک
9. **correctly**
   به درستی
10. **badly**
    بدی

Section B — Make a sentence

How does he <u>sing the song</u>?

He sings the song <u>beautifully</u>.

He doesn't sing the song <u>badly</u>.

How do they <u>play the guitar</u>?

They play the guitar <u>loudly</u>.

They don't play the guitar <u>correctly</u>.

Learn: sing the song, play the piano, play the violin, play the cello, play the drums, play the guitar

Section C — Make a question

Does she <u>play the violin</u> <u>gracefully</u>?
Yes, she does. / No, she doesn't.

Do you <u>play the drums</u> <u>well</u>?
Yes, I do. / No, I don't.

Alternative: **Yes, I play the drums well.**

Section D — Learn a verb

notice – noticing – noticed – noticed توجه کردن

You will **notice** that my family speaks loudly.

I'm **noticing** more and more how well she speaks English.

I **noticed** you haven't done your homework correctly.

She hadn't **noticed** her friend looking at her.

Section E — Learn an idiom

Music to one's ears

Meaning: Something very pleasing to hear.

"It was *music to my ears* when I heard that the teacher cancelled the test!"

Section F Write

Trace and fill in the words

1. How _____ _____ play _____ piano?

   She _____ the _____ _____.

2. _____ do we _____ the _____?

   _____ play _____ violin _____.

3. How _____ _____ play _____ cello?

   He _____ the _____ _____.

4. _____ _____ you _____ the _____?

   _____ _____ the drums _____.

5. Does _____ play the _____ _____?

   _____, he _____ _____ trumpet correctly.

6. _____ you _____ the song beautifully?

   No, _____ _____.

7. _____ she _____ the _____ well?

   Yes, _____ play _____ cello _____.

8. _____ _____ play _____ guitar _____?

   No, they _____.

Section G — Let's have fun

Music!

Write the correct verb

1. **play/plays?** He _____ the piano beautifully.

2. **sing/sings?** She _____ the song quietly.

3. **play/plays?** They _____ the violin badly.

4. **play/plays?** We _____ the guitar well.

Write the sentences

1. plays the piano - quick

   She plays the piano quickly.

2. sings the song - beautiful

   _____.

3. plays the trumpet - loud

   _____.

4. plays the cello - bad

   _____.

Lesson 43: Feelings

احساسات

How have you been feeling lately?
Lately, I've been feeling tired.

Section A | Words

1. sad
غمگین
2. tired
خسته
3. fine
خوب
4. bored
بی حوصله
5. energetic
پر انرژی

6. happy
خوشحال
7. sick
بیمار
8. angry
خشمگین
9. excited
برانگیخته
10. frustrated
ناامید

Section B | Make a sentence

How have you been feeling lately?

Lately, I've been feeling <u>sad</u>.

I haven't been feeling <u>energetic</u>.

How are you now?

I'm <u>happy</u>.

I'm not <u>frustrated</u>.

Note: I've = I have / she's = she has / he's = he has
they've = they have / we've = we have / you've = you have

Section C — Make a question

Have you been feeling <u>tired</u> lately?

Yes, I have been. / No, I haven't been.

Are you <u>angry</u>?

Yes, I am. / No, I'm not.

Alternative: **Yes, I am angry.**

Section D — Learn a verb

think – thinking – thought – thought فکر کردن

I **think** she feels fine now. Thank you for your concern.

She's frustrated because she keeps **thinking** about work.

Peter **thought** about how excited his child was to see him.

I haven't **thought** about this before.

Section E — Learn an idiom

Mixed Feelings

Meaning: When you are not sure about how you feel about something.

"He had *mixed feelings* about moving to a new city."

| Section F | Write |

Trace and fill in the words

1. _____ have _____ been _____ _____ ?
   Lately, I've _____ feeling _____ .

2. How _____ she _____ feeling _____ ?
   _____ , _____ been _____ _____ .

3. _____ _____ they been _____ lately?
   Lately, _____ _____ _____ bored.

4. How _____ he _____ feeling _____ ?
   Lately, _____ been _____ _____ .

5. _____ you _____ feeling _____ lately?
   _____ , _____ haven't _____ .

6. _____ he been _____ _____ lately?
   _____ , _____ has _____ .

7. Have _____ _____ feeling _____ lately?
   _____ , I _____ been.

8. _____ he been _____ sick _____ ?
   No, _____ _____ _____ .

198

Section G   Let's have fun

Feelings!

Match the face with the word

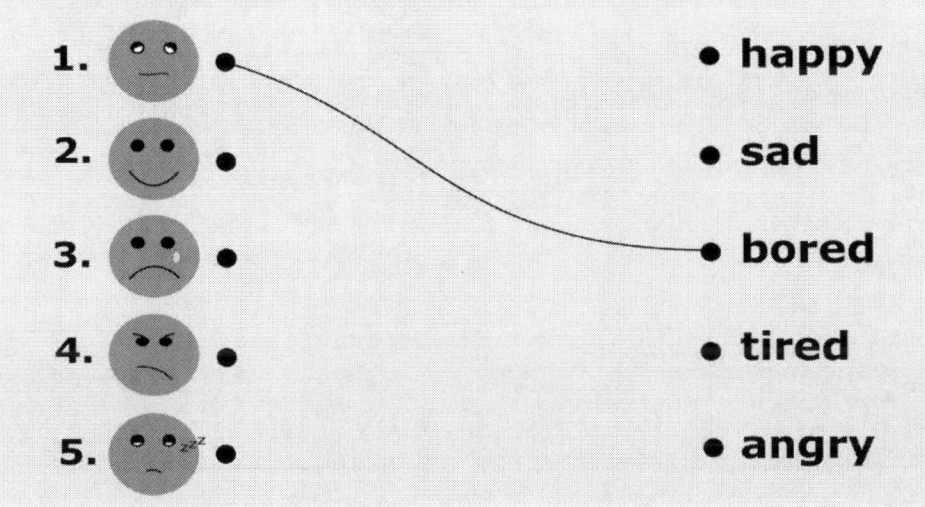

1. — bored
2. — happy
3. — sad
4. — angry
5. — tired

Answer the questions

1. How has he been feeling lately?
   <u>Lately, he's been feeling bored</u>.

2. How has she been feeling lately?
   _____.

3. How have they been feeling lately?
   _____.

4. Has she been feeling tired lately?
   _____.

5. Has he been feeling angry lately?
   _____.

How have you been feeling lately?

_____.

Lesson 44: The calendar

تقویم

> When is your competition?
> My competition is on the 2nd of May.

Section A — Words

1. **birthday**
   روز تولد
2. **competition**
   رقابت -مسابقه
3. **class**
   کلاس
4. **speech**
   سخنرانی
5. **party**
   جشن ,مهمانی
6. **meeting**
   ملاقات
7. **appointment**
   وقت ملاقات
8. **test**
   تست
9. **day off**
   مرخصی روزانه
10. **recital**
    رسیتال

Section B — Make a sentence

When is your <u>birthday</u>?

My birthday is on the <u>21st</u> of <u>February</u>.

My birthday isn't on the <u>3rd</u> of <u>December</u>.

Learn: January, February, March, April, May, June, July, August, September, October, November, December

1st 2nd 3rd 4th 5th 6th 7th 8th 9th 10th 11th 12th 13th 14th 15th 16th 17th 18th 19th 20th 21st 22nd 23rd 24th 25th 26th 27th 28th 29th 30th 31st

Section C — Make a question

Is your <u>meeting</u> on the <u>12th</u> of <u>November</u>?

Yes, it is. / No, it isn't.

Was your <u>party</u> on the <u>10th</u> of <u>June</u>?

Yes, it was. / No, it wasn't.

Alternative: **Yes, it was on the 10th of June.**

Section D — Learn a verb

organize – organizing – organized – organized سازماندهی کردن

She will **organize** a meeting for this Friday.

Fran is **organizing** a person to help me with the recital.

The teacher **organized** a speech competition at school.

She has **organized** many parties for the company.

Section E — Learn an idiom

Make a date

Meaning: To arrange a meeting with someone.

"We should *make a date* and discuss this further."

Section F — Write

Trace and fill in the words

1. _____ is _____ appointment?

   My _____ is _____ the _____ of September.

2. When _____ _____ competition?

   His _____ _____ on the 31st _____ _____.

3. _____ is their _____?

   _____ test _____ on _____ 11th of _____.

4. When _____ _____ party?

   Her _____ is _____ _____ 12th of _____.

5. _____ your _____ on the 15th of _____?

   No, _____ isn't.

6. Was _____ speech _____ the 18th of _____?

   No, it _____.

7. Is her day off _____ the _____ of _____?

   Yes, _____ _____.

8. Was their class _____ the _____ _____ May?

   _____, it _____.

Section G — Let's have fun

The calendar!

May

Monday	Tuesday	Wednesday	Thursday	Friday	Saturday	Sunday
	1st	2nd	3rd	4th Meeting	5th	6th
7th	8th Recital	9th	10th	11th	12th	13th
14th	15th	16th	17th Birthday	18th	19th	20th
21st	22nd Test	23rd	24th	25th	26th Party	27th
28th Day off	29th	30th	31st			

Answer the questions

1. When is your birthday?

   _____.

2. When is your test?

   _____.

3. Is your party on the 26th of May?

   _____.

4. Was your test on the 22nd of April?

   _____.

Test 11 — Lesson 41 - 44

Write the answer next to the letter "A"

A: ___ 1. ___ was the horror movie ___ ? It was scary.

a. How, like   b. When, see   c. Where, like   d. What, like

A: ___ 2. Was the comedy as funny ___ the action movie?

a. movie   b. watch   c. like   d. as

A: ___ 3. His mother ___ how to swim.

a. teach him   b. taught him   c. teaches he   d. learn him

A: ___ 4. "Her speech was great. It will be a tough ___ to follow."

a. day   b. act   c. song   d. beat

A: ___ 5. She ___ the piano ___ every Saturday night.

a. plays, well   b. play, quickly   c. playing, slowly   d. play, bad

A: ___ 6. Does he ___ the drums ___ for this song?

a. play, correctly   b. play, good   c. plays, well   d. plays, badly

A: ___ 7. He hadn't ___ his friend speaking Chinese to him.

a. notice   b. notices   c. noticed   d. noticing

A: ___ 8. "It's such good news! It's ___ to my ears."

a. singing   b. dancing   c. sound   d. music

A: ___ **9.** Lately, she ___ been ___ happy.

a. have, feeling   b. is, felt   c. has, feeling   d. does, feels

A: ___ **10.** ___ you been feeling ___ lately? No, I haven't been.

a. Do, tired   b. Can, tired   c. Have, tired   d. Have, tire

A: ___ **11.** Todd wasn't ___ excited during gym class yesterday.

a. feeling   b. feel   c. feels   d. felt

A: ___ **12.** "He wasn't sure what to do. He had ___ feelings."

a. mixing   b. mixed   c. mix   d. mixes

A: ___ **13.** When is ___ birthday? His birthday is on ___ 10th of May.

a. him, it   b. he's, a   c. he's, one   d. his, the

A: ___ **14.** Is ___ recital on the 15th of November? No, it ___.

a. her, isn't   b. his, doesn't   c. your, can't   d. my, won't

A: ___ **15.** Fran is ___ a group of people to help us.

a. organize   b. organizing   c. organizes   d. organized

A: ___ **16.** "Let's arrange a meeting. We should make a ___."

a. meet   b. test   c. date   d. try

Answers on page 206

Answers — Test 1 - 11

Test 1
1. a 2. c 3. a 4. d 5. d 6. c 7. c 8. b 9. d 10. b 11. b 12. a 13. a 14. a 15. c 16. d

Test 2
1. b 2. c 3. c 4. d 5. a 6. b 7. d 8. b 9. d 10. a 11. c 12. c 13. d 14. c 15. b 16. d

Test 3
1. d 2. b 3. d 4. c 5. b 6. a 7. c 8. a 9. d 10. c 11. c 12. d 13. a 14. c 15. c 16. d

Test 4
1. d 2. b 3. c 4. c 5. d 6. d 7. a 8. d 9. b 10. b 11. c 12. b 13. d 14. d 15. a 16. d

Test 5
1. a 2. a 3. c 4. b 5. d 6. d 7. b 8. a 9. c 10. d 11. c 12. b 13. d 14. c 15. a 16. c

Test 6
1. b 2. b 3. a 4. d 5. c 6. c 7. d 8. b 9. a 10. d 11. a 12. b 13. b 14. c 15. c 16. c

Test 7
1. c 2. c 3. b 4. a 5. b 6. a 7. c 8. d 9. d 10. c 11. a 12. c 13. b 14. b 15. d 16. d

Test 8
1. a 2. b 3. c 4. d 5. c 6. b 7. d 8. a 9. d 10. b 11. c 12. a 13. d 14. b 15. c 16. a

Test 9
1. b 2. c 3. c 4. a 5. d 6. d 7. a 8. b 9. d 10. a 11. c 12. b 13. b 14. a 15. c 16. d

Test 10
1. b 2. d 3. a 4. c 5. d 6. c 7. a 8. b 9. a 10. d 11. b 12. c 13. b 14. d 15. c 16. a

Test 11
1. d 2. d 3. b 4. b 5. a 6. a 7. c 8. d 9. c 10. c 11. a 12. b 13. d 14. a 15. b 16. c

Preston Lee's other great books!

Preston Lee's Beginner English

Preston Lee's Beginner English For Persian Speakers (44 Lessons)
Preston Lee's Beginner English Lesson 1 – 60 For Persian Speakers
Preston Lee's Beginner English Lesson 1 – 80 For Persian Speakers
Preston Lee's Beginner English 100 Lessons For Persian Speakers

- **Preston Lee's Beginner English 20 Lesson Series**

Preston Lee's Beginner English Lesson 1 – 20 For Persian Speakers
Preston Lee's Beginner English Lesson 21 – 40 For Persian Speakers
Preston Lee's Beginner English Lesson 41 – 60 For Persian Speakers
Preston Lee's Beginner English Lesson 61 – 80 For Persian Speakers

Preston Lee's Intermediate English

Preston Lee's Intermediate English Lesson 1 – 40 For Persian Speakers
Preston Lee's Intermediate English Lesson 1 – 60 For Persian Speakers
Preston Lee's Intermediate English Lesson 1 – 80 For Persian Speakers
Preston Lee's Intermediate English 100 Lessons For Persian Speakers

- **Preston Lee's Beginner English 20 Lesson Series**

Preston Lee's Intermediate English Lesson 1 – 20 For Persian Speakers
Preston Lee's Intermediate English Lesson 21 – 40 For Persian Speakers

Preston Lee's Conversation English

Preston Lee's Conversation English Lesson 1 – 40 For Persian Speakers
Preston Lee's Conversation English Lesson 1 – 60 For Persian Speakers
Preston Lee's Conversation English 100 Lessons For Persian Speakers

- **Preston Lee's Conversation English 20 Lesson Series**

Preston Lee's Conversation English Lesson 1 – 20 For Persian Speakers
Preston Lee's Conversation English Lesson 21 – 40 For Persian Speakers
Preston Lee's Conversation English Lesson 41 – 60 For Persian Speakers

Preston Lee's Read & Write English

Preston Lee's Read & Write English Lesson 1 – 40 For Persian Speakers
Preston Lee's Read & Write English Lesson 1 – 60 For Persian Speakers

- **Preston Lee's Read & Write English 20 Lesson Series**

Preston Lee's Read & Write English Lesson 1 – 20 For Persian Speakers
Preston Lee's Read & Write English Lesson 21 – 40 For Persian Speakers
Preston Lee's Read & Write English Lesson 41 – 60 For Persian Speakers

Preston Lee's Beginner English Words

Preston Lee's Beginner English 500 Words For Persian Speakers
Preston Lee's Beginner English 800 Words For Persian Speakers
Preston Lee's Beginner English 1000 Words For Persian Speakers

Preston Lee's Master English Speaking

Preston Lee's Master English Speaking - Volume 1
Preston Lee's Master English Speaking - Volume 2
Preston Lee's Master English Speaking - Volume 1 – 2
Preston Lee's Master English Speaking - Volume 3
Preston Lee's Master English Speaking - Volume 4
Preston Lee's Master English Speaking - Volume 3 – 4
Preston Lee's Master English Speaking - Volume 1 – 4

Made in United States
Troutdale, OR
10/11/2023